Life in the
THIRTEEN COLONIES

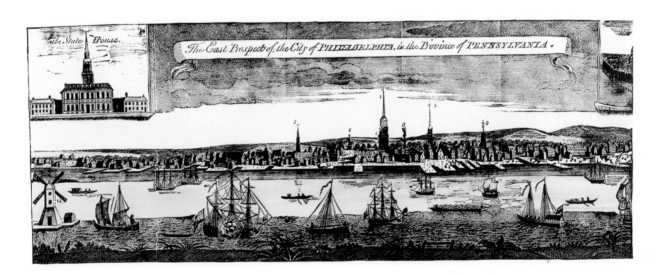

The East Prospect of the City of PHILADELPHIA, in the Province of PENNSYLVANIA.

the State House.

Pennsylvania

Deborah H. DeFord

children's press®
An imprint of
SCHOLASTIC

Library of Congress Cataloging-in-Publication Data

DeFord, Deborah H.
  Pennsylvania / by Deborah H. DeFord.
     p. cm. — (Life in the thirteen colonies)
  Includes bibliographical references and index.
  ISBN 0-516-24577-5
  1. Pennsylvania—History—Colonial period, ca. 1600–1775—Juvenile literature. 2. Pennsylvania—
History—Revolution, 1775–1783—Juvenile literature. I. Title. II. Series.
  F152.D34 2004
  974.8'02—dc22

                              2004001943

1 2 3 4 5 6 7 8 9 10 R 13 12 11 10 09 08 07 06 05 04

A Creative Media Applications Production
Design: Fabia Wargin Design
Editor: Laura Walsh
Copy Editor: Laurie Lieb
Proofreader: Tania Bissell
Content Research: Lauren Thogersen
Photo Researcher: Annette Cyr
Content Consultant: David Silverman, Ph.D.

Photo Credits © 2004

Title page © North Wind Archives; p. 2 © Archivo Iconografico, S.A./CORBIS; p. 4 © Bettmann/CORBIS; p. 7 © Getty
Images/Hulton Archive; p. 11 © North Wind Archives; p. 20 © North Wind Archives; p. 21 © Getty Images/Hulton Archive;
p. 25 © Getty Images/Hulton Archive; p. 28 © Bettmann/CORBIS; p. 30 © North Wind Archives; p. 35 © John
Bartholomew/CORBIS; p. 36 © Bob Rowan; Progressive Image/CORBIS; p. 36 © Philadelphia Museum of Art/CORBIS; p.
39 © North Wind Archives; p. 41 © Getty Images/Hulton Archive; p. 44 © Getty Images/Hulton Archive; p. 47 © North
Wind Archives; p. 48 © Bettmann/CORBIS; p. 50 © Getty Images/Hulton Archive; p. 54 © North Wind Archive; p. 57 ©
North Wind Archives; p. 60 Top right © Getty Images/Hulton Archive; Bottom left © Bowers Museum of Cultural
Art/CORBIS; Bottom right © Getty Images/Hulton Archives; p. 61 Top left © Getty Images/Hulton Archives; Top right ©
Getty Images/Hulton Archive; Center left © Getty Images/Hulton Archive; Center (arrowheads) © Andy Angstrom; Bottom
right (stone adze) © Ulster County Historical Society; Center right © Nathan Benn/CORBIS; Bottom right © Getty
Images/Hulton Archive; p. 62 © North Wind Archives; p. 63 © North Wind Archives; p. 65 © North Wind Archives; p. 71 ©
North Wind Archives; p. 74 © North Wind Archives; p. 77 © North Wind Archives; p. 78 © G.E. Kidder Smith/CORBIS; p.
81 © Bettmann/CORBIS; p. 82 © Philadelphia Museum of Art/CORBIS; p. 84 © North Wind Archives; p. 88 ©
Bettmann/CORBIS; p. 90 © North Wind Archives; p. 93 © North Wind Archives; p. 98 © North Wind Archives; p. 102 ©
Bettmann/CORBIS; p. 104 © North Wind Archives; p. 108 © Getty Images/Hulton Archive; p. 109 © North Wind Archives;
p. 111 © North Wind Archives; p. 115 © Getty Images/Hulton Archive; p. 117 © Philadelphia Museum of Art/CORBIS; p.
118 Top left © Bettmann/CORBIS; p. 118 Top right © Getty Images/Hulton Archive; p. 118 Bottom left © North Wind
Archives; p. 118 Bottom right © Bettmann/CORBIS; p. 119 Top © Bettmann/CORBIS; p. 119 Bottom left © North Wind
Archives; p. 119 Bottom right © North Wind Archives

CONTENTS

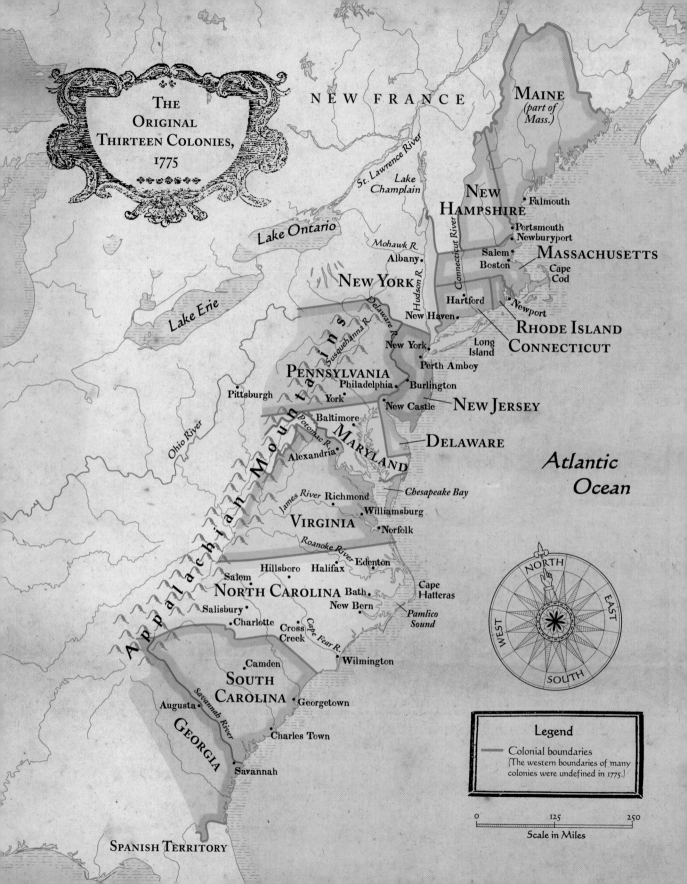

THE
ORIGINAL
THIRTEEN COLONIES,
1775

NEW FRANCE

MAINE
(part of
Mass.)

St. Lawrence River

Lake
Champlain

NEW
HAMPSHIRE

Falmouth

Portsmouth
Newburyport

Lake Ontario

Mohawk R.

Albany

Connecticut River

Salem
Boston

MASSACHUSETTS

Cape
Cod

NEW YORK

Hudson R.

Hartford

Newport

Lake Erie

Delaware R.

New Haven

RHODE ISLAND
CONNECTICUT

Susquehanna R.

New York

Long
Island

Appalachian Mountains

PENNSYLVANIA

Perth Amboy

Philadelphia

Burlington

Pittsburgh

York

New Castle

NEW JERSEY

Ohio River

Baltimore

Potomac R.

MARYLAND

DELAWARE

Alexandria

Atlantic
Ocean

James River

Richmond

Chesapeake Bay

Williamsburg

VIRGINIA

Norfolk

Roanoke River

Edenton

Hillsboro

Halifax

Cape
Hatteras

Salem

NORTH CAROLINA

Bath

Salisbury

New Bern

Pamlico
Sound

Charlotte

Cross
Creek

Cape Fear R.

Wilmington

Camden

NORTH

SOUTH
CAROLINA

Georgetown

WEST

EAST

Augusta

Savannah River

GEORGIA

Charles Town

SOUTH

Savannah

Legend

Colonial boundaries
(The western boundaries of many
colonies were undefined in 1775.)

SPANISH TERRITORY

0   125   250

Scale in Miles

A Nation Grows
From Thirteen Colonies

Pennsylvania lies in the mid-Atlantic region of the United States. It is bordered by New York, New Jersey, Delaware, Maryland, West Virginia, and Ohio. It was one of the original thirteen colonies.

The first Europeans to visit Pennsylvania encountered many Indian tribes living along the Delaware River and deep in the forests.

The British claimed Pennsylvania, and gave the land to William Penn. He built a colony based on religious freedom. People of many backgrounds flocked to Pennsylvania.

Pennsylvania's largest city, Philadelphia, became the center of the American Revolution. The Declaration of Independence and U.S. **Constitution** first took shape there. The Liberty Bell still hangs there as a reminder of the freedom all Americans enjoy

The map shows the thirteen English colonies in 1775. The colored sections show the areas that were settled at that time.

CHAPTER ONE

Discovery

The First Arrival

It was 1609 when the explorer Henry Hudson guided his ship, the *Half Moon*, into what is now Delaware Bay. The bay stretched inland to the Delaware River and north to what would become the colony of Pennsylvania. As the large, painted vessel glided along the shoreline, the native people who lived there must have watched in amazement. No European ship had ever sailed into this bay before.

Hudson had been hired by the Dutch East India Company in the Netherlands to find a water route across North America to connect the Atlantic Ocean and the Pacific Ocean. This water route was called the Northwest Passage. No one really knew if it existed or not.

The Dutch East India Company, like many other companies in Europe, **imported** fine silks, gold, jewels, and rare spices from Asia to sell in Europe. The land and water

⌐ The European ships were beautifully decorated. The local Native Americans had never seen anything quite like them.

routes that the company's traders traveled to bring Asian goods to Europe were long, slow, and dangerous. A Northwest Passage would make the trip faster. This meant that the company would have goods to sell more often, which would mean more profits.

Hudson soon realized that the river leading into Delaware Bay was not the passage he was looking for. Even so, when he returned to the Netherlands, he talked about what he had seen in America. He described the American Indians and their skill at hunting. He also described the huge numbers of animals that could provide valuable furs and skins to sell for high prices in Europe.

Henry Hudson and his party are met by Native Americans as they come ashore to explore the new land.

Dutch Settlement

The Dutch East India Company began to see that America might have riches of its own, so it decided to form a new trading company called the Dutch West India Company. This company sent traders to deal with the native people, such as the Lenni-Lenape, whom Hudson had seen on the banks of Delaware Bay.

The Dutch traders brought to America many items that the natives had never seen before. The traders explained that the natives should bring furs to the trading posts. In exchange, the Indians would receive firewater (alcohol), steel axes, iron pots, cheap cloth, and other European goods.

Unlike some Native American tribes, the Lenni-Lenape helped the European people who settled on their traditional hunting grounds. Other tribes reacted with fear or anger when Europeans came to their land, either keeping their distance or attacking the settlers. The Lenni-Lenape were part of a friendly tribe that had also made peace with other Indian tribes, especially the Iroquois. The Iroquois included five tribes who shared the same language and traditions. They controlled much of the territory around what would later become Pennsylvania.

The "Original People"

The tribal name Lenni-Lenape means "original people." The Europeans called the tribe the Delaware Indians, using the European name given to the bay and river. Settlers often chose their own names to use instead of native names, probably because they found their European words easier to pronounce.

The Lenni-Lenape continued to live in their traditional ways, despite their new European neighbors. In their small villages, the Lenni-Lenape built structures called longhouses. These were log buildings 30 to 110 feet (9 to 33 meters) long and 20 feet (6 meters) wide, covered inside and out with bark. A single longhouse held as many as ten families, all related to the eldest woman.

In a longhouse, the women tended their children, prepared food on a central fire, and made the utensils and clothing their families needed. Part of the house was separated into rooms for individual families. On high shelves, they stored clay or wooden pots and bowls, mats, baskets, and buckets made of bark for storing food and carrying water. They also stored tobacco and pipes for their tribal ceremonies.

The women owned all the tribe's property and decided which men would be made chiefs. The chiefs led councils, where the tribe's spiritual leaders and older members met. The chiefs, representing the tribe, met with other tribes or with the European settlers.

The Lenni-Lenape had simple laws. They considered stealing and harming others to be major crimes. When people broke these laws, either the chief or the council would decide on their punishment. This simple system helped the Lenni-Lenape avoid **feuds** among themselves.

The Lenni-Lenape had great respect for their land. They harvested, hunted, and fished only for what they needed to survive.

Food in the Village

Lenni-Lenape men fished and hunted for game animals, such as deer, buffalo, and rabbit. The people ate any animals that could be hunted, except bats and mice. A meal might include opossum, porcupine, raccoon, ground-hog, beaver, muskrat, or even wildcat. The natives also ate frogs, turtles, and rattlesnakes. The Lenni-Lenape considered it a special treat to cook up the noisy insect later known as the cicada.

The women planted pumpkins, squash, corn, and beans. They gathered apples, berries, and nuts from the wild. Women and men, young and old, knew how to catch fish, either with a basket or a spear. The Lenni-Lenape also made sugar and syrup with sap taken from the forest trees.

The most important part of the Lenni-Lenape's diet was corn. They boiled, ground, or roasted the corn and prepared it with meat, fish, nuts, or maple sugar. A corn crop, however, quickly uses up the nutrients in the soil where it is planted. When this happened, the people moved to a new location where the fresh soil would produce a healthy crop.

Native Culture

Religion was an important part of Lenni-Lenape life. The tribe's spiritual leaders were older men who told the traditional stories of their religion. The natives believed in one god, the creator of all things, whom they called the Great Spirit. They had no written scripture or particular way to practice their faith, yet they all prayed to the Great Spirit. They believed that all the things they found in nature, including rocks, trees, animals, and rivers, had souls and should be treated with respect. Every fall, the people gathered to thank the Great Spirit for the summer's crops and to ask for mercy through the winter to come.

Lenni-Lenape children did not attend school. They learned to hunt, farm, and continue the traditions of their people by working alongside their elders and listening to the elders' stories. The arrival of the Europeans would bring great changes to the simple village life of the Native Americans. However, in the early days of European settlement, the Lenni-Lenape had no way of knowing how different their future would be.

The First Colonists

The Dutch traders were just one of many groups of Europeans who would come to the land of the Lenni-Lenape. In Pennsylvania, more than in other colonies, people came from a number of different European countries. Each group brought its own language and traditions. Because of their differences, the different peoples often created settlements apart from other groups.

Thanks to Hudson's reports about the new land, the Dutch arrived first. A growing number of Dutch fur traders set up forts that they used as trading posts along the Delaware River. These men did not want to make homes in the New World. They came to the New World simply to trade and make money. (To the Europeans, their homelands in Europe made up the Old World. The lands of the Americas were the New World.)

Next to arrive were people from Sweden and Finland. They were the first Europeans to arrive in family groups, intending to live in what is now Pennsylvania. In 1638, two Swedish ships, the *Kalmar Nyckel* and the *Grippen,* tied up along the Delaware River. The settlers, both Swedes and Finns, rowed to shore in smaller boats, carrying their supplies with them. Their leader, Peter Minuit, was ready to start a settlement. Minuit was no stranger to America.

He had once been the governor of the Dutch colony of New Netherland, which later became New York.

The first thing Minuit did was to meet with a local council of Native Americans and buy land for the new settlement. Next, the settlers built Fort Christina, where weapons were stored and where the people could take shelter in case of attack by unfriendly tribes or other Europeans. Minuit then sailed for Sweden, intending to bring more settlers back to Pennsylvania. However, his ship went down in a storm, and he drowned.

As more Swedish families arrived in the New World, they established themselves by building homes, churches, and, later on, schools.

The Swedes Settle In

In 1640, two more Swedish expeditions arrived, bringing more settlers, supplies, farm animals, and a minister. Most of the land of Pennsylvania was covered with forest. Because the Finns and Swedes came from heavily forested lands, they knew how to turn forests into farms. Using axes and other tools brought from their homeland, they chopped down trees and turned them into logs to build America's first log cabins.

Three years later, a Swedish military man named Johan Printz arrived from Sweden with still more settlers. He established a new town and became governor of the growing colony called New Sweden. Printz's town was the first permanent European settlement in what would become Pennsylvania.

The Swedes lived in peace with both the Dutch and the Native Americans in the region. Soon, the Swedes got involved in the fur trade that the Dutch had started. As the Swedes got to know the Lenni-Lenape, they realized how skilled the Indians were at farming. Before long, they had learned from the Native Americans how to grow corn, beans, squash, tomatoes, and tobacco on their new land.

A Land of Plenty

The settlers had all kinds of trees available to them. Many different hardwood trees, such as oaks, chestnuts, and maples, grew in the southern parts of the region. In northern parts, where the land was higher and rockier, pines, hemlocks, and other evergreens grew. The wood from the trees made it possible to build homes and fences and make needed tools. The settlers also used the wood as fuel for their fires and then made the ashes into **potash**, which was used to make soap. Tree bark was handy for tanning leather, a process that made animal skins soft enough to use for clothing and other items.

Like their Indian neighbors, the settlers depended on many wild animals for food. They hunted wild turkeys, ducks, geese, quail, grouse, and other birds. Pigeons became such a popular meal that they were hunted almost to extinction. Deer and elk provided warm, sturdy skins from which to make clothing. Animals such as beavers, foxes, bears, raccoon, and otters were prized for their valuable furs.

Some animals were dangerous. The settlers learned to defend themselves and their livestock against mountain lions (also called panthers, cougars, or pumas) and bears. For protection, they built tall fences of upright logs around their settlements. The animals of the forest lived right outside these walls.

Letters from the colonists to their friends and families in Europe described the misery of pesky mosquitoes, midges, and bedbugs. The settlers also wrote of dragonflies, mayflies, and wasps. The colonists saw their very first fireflies, which did not exist in Europe. On the other hand, the earliest settlers brought a newcomer, the honeybee, with them to the New World. Honeybees soon escaped into the wild and multiplied. Both settlers and Native Americans used the wild honey they found in hollow buttonwood trees.

Honeybees in the New World

Colonists transported hives of honeybees across the ocean in hollow logs or woven straw domes called skeps. They used the bees' honey in bread, porridge, and beverages. They also used it to preserve fruit and make medicines, cement, and furniture polish. When the skeps became too crowded, some of the bees swarmed away to make new homes in the wild.

In *Letters from an American Farmer,* J. Hector St. John de Crèvecoeur wrote about "hunting" for wild bees:

"I make a small fire…[and] on the fire I put some wax," he wrote. "On another stone, I drop honey in distinct drops, which I surround with small quantities of vermillion [a bright red substance thought to attract bees]."

The smell of the hot wax drew the bees to the honey. While gathering honey to take back to their wild hives, the bees got vermillion on their bodies. This dyed them red. Crèvecoeur used his compass to see which way the red-marked bees flew. Then he followed his compass to find them.

A Fight for Ownership

While New Sweden was being settled, the Dutch were creating their own settlement called New Amsterdam (later New York) to the north. The Dutch government claimed that its people were the only ones who had a right to the fur trade in the area. They would not let the Swedish take any furs for their own. In 1654, Dutch soldiers marched to New Sweden and forced the Swedish settlers to hand over control of the colony. About 400 Swedes stayed, even though they would have to live under the new Dutch government. The rest sailed back to Europe.

In the meantime, the English had been busy exploring and making their own settlements in America. By 1655, they had created ten colonies with thousands of settlers. However, they wanted more colonies, including the Dutch colonies in Pennsylvania.

In 1664, English **troops** peacefully captured the Dutch trading posts and the former settlement of New Sweden. The English told the people there that they would now be colonists of England. A handful of English settlers then arrived and made Upland (later Chester, Pennsylvania) the capital of the colony. The entire European population of Pennsylvania, including Dutch, Swedes, and English, was still very small. That would change when William Penn arrived.

Lake Ontario

Lake Erie

NORTH

WEST

EAST

SOUTH

PENNSYLVANIA,
1775

NEW YORK

Presque Isle

Susquehanna River

Allegheny River

Shenango River

Clarion River

Delaware River

Susquehanna River

Trenton

Lehigh River

Easton

PENNSYLVANIA

• Kittanning

West Branch Susquehanna River

Juniata River

Bethlehem

Conemaugh River

Reading •

A p p a l a c h i a n   M o u n t a i n s

Ohio River

Fort Pitt
(Pittsburgh)

Ephrata •

Valley
Forge •

Lancaster •

Philadephia
Chester •

Germantown

Fort Christina ◇

**NEW
JERSEY**

MARYLAND

Delaware Bay

DELAWARE

VIRGINIA

Legend
— Colonial boundaries
(The western boundaries of many
colonies were undefined in 1775.)

0   25   50
Scale in Miles

CHAPTER TWO

The Holy Experiment in Penn's Woods

Penn and the Quakers

William Penn was an Englishman who belonged to a religious group called the Society of Friends, also known as the Quakers. Penn and his fellow Quakers disagreed strongly with what was taught in the official Church of England and refused to follow its teachings. The leaders of the Church of England insisted that everyone must do as the church said. As far as they were concerned, the Quakers were troublemakers. Penn, like many other Quakers, was put in prison many times for promoting Quaker ideas through his writings and speeches.

🖎 *This map shows how Pennsylvania looked in 1775.*

In 1681, Penn asked King Charles II of England to grant him a **charter** for a new colony in America. The charter would give Penn ownership of the colony. He would be able to decide who would live there and how they would live. Charles II did not think much of Penn because of his Quaker beliefs. However, the king had been friends with Penn's father, so he agreed to Penn's request. The king named the new colony Pennsylvania, which is Latin for "Penn's Woods." In Pennsylvania, Penn wanted Quakers and others to be able to practice their religion freely. His new colony, he said, would be "a free colony for all mankind," a "holy experiment."

Creating a New Colony

Before Penn traveled to America, he sent a letter to the 2,000 Dutch and Swedish colonists already living on the land the king had given him. "It hath pleased God," Penn wrote, "to cast you in my lot and care." If he wanted his plans for a new colony to work, he would need to make these colonists his friends.

Penn also needed to create a local government and plan towns for the colony. Most of all, he had to attract settlers who would build towns, farms, and businesses. Only then would his colony prosper. So Penn wrote exciting brochures to make people want to join his "holy experiment."

Pennsylvania, Penn wrote, was "600 miles [960 kilometers] nearer the Sun than England," with plenty of wildlife and rich farmland. He promised to let people either rent land for "one penny per acre" or purchase 50 acres (20 hectares) per household member.

The Quakers

The Quakers believe in God and that God speaks to every person individually. All a person needs to do is believe and obey. Anyone can stand up in a Quaker meeting to say what God has spoken to him or her. In the Church of England, only the priests and bishops could speak. They taught that God speaks only through the words of the Christian Bible.

Quakers also believe that war is wrong. They are **pacifists**, or people who are opposed to violence for any reason. They refuse to fight under any circumstances, even when a king or government tells them they must. They believe that all people are equal, as well. In Penn's time, they refused to follow the English practice of removing their hats or bowing to officials. They dressed plainly, instead of dressing in styles that showed whether they were rich or poor, as most people did. In addition, the Quakers disapproved of singing, dancing, theater, and sports.

England's leaders, fearing that the Quakers would teach others to disobey the church and the king, punished the Quakers for their beliefs. In the twenty years before Penn's charter, the English government sent more than 10,000 Quakers to prison and sentenced 250 Quakers to death. The Quakers did not leave England only for the freedom to worship as they believed. They felt they were running for their lives.

Traveling to America

It took a lot of courage to sail from Europe across the wide Atlantic Ocean to America. The voyage could take anywhere from three weeks to two months. Along the way, the ship might encounter enemy warships, pirates, storms, shipwrecks, or disease. Many people became seasick. They were called "puke-stockings" by the sailors aboard. With so many people vomiting, the ships usually smelled horrible.

One hundred passengers sailed to Pennsylvania with William Penn on the ship *Welcome*. The trip took nearly two months, and many of the passengers spent most of their time on the "'tween deck," a low-ceilinged space inside the ship. All they had to eat was salt pork and beef, hard sea biscuits, and dried beans and peas. In good weather, they cooked the food on the ship's hearth (fireplace) or on small iron stoves

Settlers who survived the trip from Europe across the Atlantic were met by a beautiful new land full of natural resources.

called cook boxes. When storms tossed the ship, the passengers ate their food cold because they did not want to risk a blaze started by an ember thrown from a cooking fire. Before long, green algae grew in the drinking water, which also collected bugs.

The water on board ship also contained germs. It was common for people on a ship to come down with diseases such as typhoid, dysentery, and smallpox. The *Welcome's* voyage was no exception. Of the hundred people who traveled with Penn, thirty contracted smallpox and died at sea.

Penn Arrives

Almost as soon as Penn arrived in his colony in October 1682, he held elections to choose the people who would form Pennsylvania's government. At the same time, he wrote something he called "the Great Law," which explained how the colony's government would be organized.

Penn got his ideas directly from Quaker teachings. The Great Law stated that each person in Pennsylvania would have personal freedom. Each person's property would be protected. All the people would be able to vote for political leaders, serve in the government, and have a trial by jury if they were accused of crimes. Punishments would be fair and would fit the crimes. In England, the rulers considered it a crime just to disagree with them. In Pennsylvania, Penn defended people's rights to disagree with the government.

William Penn had a vision for a government that maintained order with equality and respect.

Penn and the Lenni-Lenape

Penn believed that the Native Americans should be treated with respect and fairness. While still in England, he had written a letter to the Lenni-Lenape in the area to make sure they knew this. He told them that he and they were equals. He wrote of the "one great God" they had in common, who "hath been pleased to make me concerned in your part of the world."

Penn knew that there had been conflict between some settlers and Native Americans. He wrote: "I am very sensible of the unkindness and injustice that hath been too much exercised toward you by the people of these parts of the world." He continued, "But I am not such a man…I desire to win and gain your love and friendship by a kind, just and peaceable life, and the people I send are of the same mind."

About the time Penn arrived in Pennsylvania in 1682, 15,000 Native Americans lived throughout the area. Penn met with the native chiefs to create a peace treaty and make several land purchases from them, even though the king of England had already given Penn the land. He later described the natives in his writings as being "generally tall, straight, well-built, and of singular proportion." He found their generosity remarkable: "Nothing is too good for a friend," he wrote. Penn also wrote that the natives were the "most merry creatures that live."

The Lenni-Lenape chief, Tammany, responded to Penn's request for peace by saying, "We will live in peace with Onas [the Indians' name for Penn] and his children as long as the sun and moon shall endure." Penn kept his promises, and the colonists lived in peace with the natives.

Wampum

When Penn and other settlers traded with the Lenape, they sometimes used wampum. These belts of polished shells were used just like money. The Indians strung the beads and made them into belts. Belts were traded by the fathom, which was a measure of length used by sailors equal to 6 feet (1.83 meters). One fathom of wampum was equal to about five British shillings in the 1700s or about $3.00 today.

The City of Brotherly Love

William Penn was a careful planner. In a pamphlet called *Brief Account,* he gave wise advice that would prepare new colonists for what lay ahead of them. He wrote, "They that go must [go] wisely and count the cost, for they must either work themselves, or be able to employ others. A winter goes before a summer, and the first work will be country labor, to clear ground, and raise provision."

Penn told future settlers what to bring with them. "All sorts of things for apparel, as cloth, stuffs, linen, etcetera." He explained that "two men may clear as much ground for corn as usually brings by the following harvest about twenty quarters [160 bushels].... And if they buy them two cows, and two breeding sows [pigs], with what the Indians for a small matter will bring in, of fowl, fish, and venison [deer meat]...that and their industry [hard work] will supply them."

Penn also carefully planned a new capital city. He named it Philadelphia, which is Greek for "city of brotherly love." On paper, he laid out the future streets in a pattern of straight lines that formed square blocks. He named many of the streets after trees, such as Chestnut, Walnut, Pine, Poplar, Apple, Quince, Peach, and Plum Street.

Soon, Penn's plans were turned into real streets and buildings. Between 1684 and 1699, the population of Philadelphia grew to 5,000. The colonists found plenty of stone for building, as well as the materials needed to make bricks and the mortar that held them together. Since Philadelphia had many buildings made of brick and stone, it had fewer fires than other cities, where most of the buildings were made of wood.

Philadelphia was a port city, located on the Delaware River, and people and goods from England arrived there by ship. Farmers traveled from their inland farms to sell their meat, grains, and produce to the city folk. Shops and other businesses opened, including inns and taverns that offered food and shelter to the city's many visitors. Sugar, molasses, spices, rum, and fine wines arrived from English colonies on the islands of the West Indies in the Caribbean Sea.

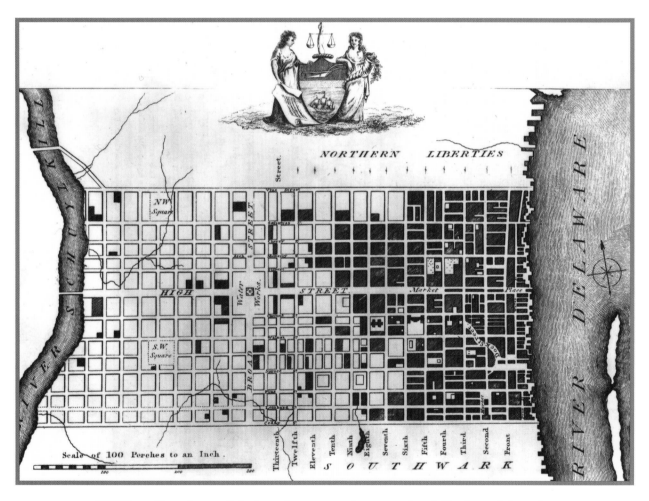

William Penn's careful planning created a port city full of wealth and diversity.

City Styles

In the early years of the city, the Quakers' plain style made Philadelphia a quiet, sober town. One visitor to a Society of Friends meeting described the scene: "There were many drab-coated men, and there were elderly women, in gowns of drab or gray, with white silk shawls and black silk-covered cardboard bonnets." Children dressed just as their parents did.

Although at first most of the people who lived in Philadelphia were Quakers, people of other religions soon joined them. Unlike the leaders of other colonies, Penn insisted that his colony would welcome people of all religions. The Anglicans (members of the Church of England) built Christ Church, which still exists today. Baptists and Presbyterians constructed meeting places of their own. Over time, other Protestant groups, as well as Jews and Catholics, arrived in the city. These different faiths lived together peacefully.

In Philadelphia, a visitor might also hear several languages spoken. Walking side by side with English-speaking people were those who spoke German, Dutch, or Welsh. Groups of people from a European country usually moved to America and settled together. They established new towns outside of Philadelphia, such as Germantown.

These groups often ran their own schools in their native languages. The Welsh actually tried to start their own colony within Pennsylvania's borders. The colony failed, but the Welsh stuck together, living in caves along the riverbanks until they could build houses.

Slaves in Philadelphia

Philadelphia's first 150 enslaved Africans arrived on the *Isabella*, a slave trader's ship, in 1684. Almost all of them remained in the city. They were brought to Pennsylvania by the Dutch and Swedes. Some Germans and English, including the Quakers, held slaves, too, even though Quaker beliefs did not support slavery. In general, Quaker opposition to slavery made it unpopular in Pennsylvania. As a result, fewer slaves worked and lived in Pennsylvania than in neighboring colonies. In 1700, a Philadelphia merchant wrote to a slave supplier "to hand me no more negroes for sale, for our people do not care to buy."

Reading and Education

Children in the early settlement years learned to read, write, and do math from their ministers or in church schools. Penn's Great Law said that all children should know how to write by the time they were twelve. Quaker education included both boys and girls, unlike education in some other colonies, where only boys attended school. In 1689, the Quakers opened Philadelphia's first Friends' public school at Fourth and Chestnut Streets.

School usually took only part of a day. Most of a child's education concentrated on the jobs of everyday life in the city or in nearby towns. The girls learned to weave, sew, garden, prepare food, and do the chores of a colonial household. Most boys followed the work of their fathers, such as building or milling. Others became **apprentices** (working students), learning a trade from a metal smith, carpenter, bricklayer, or other skilled local craftsman.

The first Quaker school was established in Pennsylvania in 1689.

Colonial Money

Just like people today, the settlers had to buy and sell goods and services to earn needed money. Gold and silver were their only money, but both were rare in the colonies. Instead, the colonists substituted "commodity money."

Commodity money included goods that were given a standard money value. For instance, a barrel of pork might equal fifty shillings. (A shilling was a British coin that would be worth about seven dollars today. A fifty-shilling barrel of pork was worth about $350.) With that barrel of pork, a person could **barter,** or trade, for anything worth fifty shillings. People might barter to put shoes on their horses, to have a field plowed, or perhaps to buy fabric or other goods. Even after the colonies created paper money, people continued to barter with commodity money.

Change on the Way

Pennsylvania grew faster than any of the other colonies. Soon, Philadelphia was the most prosperous city in the New World. Penn's clever advertising and careful planning had paid off. In the coming years, thousands of newcomers would arrive from England, Germany, France, Switzerland, and Ireland. Ship after ship would sail up the Delaware River to Philadelphia's docks. Each one of those ships would be filled with people looking for the good life Penn had promised.

CHAPTER THREE

"The Best Poor Man's Country"

The Colony Grows

Colonists sent letters with every ship that traveled from Pennsylvania to England, describing the colony as "the best poor man's country in the world." They wrote that even people who had nothing when they arrived could find plenty of cheap land and the freedom to live as they wanted.

By 1700, Penn's efforts had brought about 20,000 immigrants to his "holy experiment." A second surge of newcomers arrived in the early 1700s. Many of these people came to be known as the Pennsylvania Dutch, even though they were actually German. The term "Dutch" probably came from the German word for their spoken language, Deutsch.

Settlers often arrived in Pennsylvania with nothing but a belief in hard work. Their courage was rewarded with the opportunity to own land of their own.

Unlike the English and Welsh Quakers, who mostly ran businesses, the new immigrants were almost all farmers. The first Germans settled Germantown, outside of Philadelphia, in 1683. By 1710, many of the immigrants had moved out into the unsettled countryside. The land was good for planting, with gentle hills and a mild climate. As the farming population grew, people had to move farther away from existing towns to find land. Soon, new towns such as Lancaster, Easton, Reading, and Bethlehem were founded to provide such goods and services. The farm families traveled regularly to these towns to meet their friends, sell their produce, and buy what they needed.

The Conestoga Wagon

The Conestoga wagon had wide wheel rims that prevented the wheels from sinking into mud. It also had a curved floor that kept the wagon's contents from sliding around as it traveled up and down hills and over ruts and bumps. Pulled by teams of four or six large horses, a Conestoga could carry 6 tons (5.4 metric tons) of goods.

Most Pennsylvania Germans painted their wagons blue with red trim, attached bells to their horses' leather bridles, and covered the wagons with white canvas to protect their loads in bad weather. In the next century, pioneers would travel west across the continent in Conestoga wagons.

Moving Inland

Before 1730, no actual roads led away from the Delaware River. Pennsylvania had few major rivers flowing west to use for transporting goods to and from Philadelphia. At first, settlers made their way slowly along the paths created by the Native Americans. Then the leaders in Philadelphia decided to build a system of roads that would connect Philadelphia with outlying areas. These roads were rough dirt tracks that quickly turned to mud in rainstorms. Despite the difficulty of traveling, the roads made it possible to transport goods to and from the country farms and towns.

Before long, German-American farmers decided that the small carts they used to transport their goods did not work well enough. They invented the Conestoga wagon to get their crops and livestock to market. Conestoga wagons became common sights along Pennsylvania's larger roads. By 1750, more than 7,000 of these wagons were in use.

The German settlers also decided that they needed better guns for hunting and for defending themselves against wild animals. European rifles took too long to load and were not accurate. German gun makers soon developed the Pennsylvania rifle, which could be loaded faster. The Pennsylvania rifle also used less powder and smaller musket balls (the ammunition that the guns fired) and did not need to be cleaned as often as a European rifle. During the 1700s, the Pennsylvania rifle was the most accurate rifle in the world.

Dangers in the Wilderness

The early settlers learned to fear the panthers that lived in the forests around them. A hundred years later, these cats were still a danger, as Pennsylvanian John Bartram describes in 1738:

[Panthers] have not yet seized any of our people, but many have been sadly frightened with them. They have pursued many men both on horseback and on foot. Many have shot them down, and others have escaped by running away. But I believe, as a panther does not much fear a single man, so he hath no great desire to seize him...if he had, running from him would be but a poor means to escape from such a nimble, strong creature, which will leap above twenty feet [6 meters] at a leap.

Barns and Houses

As soon as they claimed their land, Pennsylvania's farmers built temporary log shelters. Then, as they plowed new fields, they dug up huge amounts of fieldstone. Over time, they replaced their first, simple homes with large houses built from the fieldstone. Families would choose a location where they could dig a cellar that contained a spring or well for water. The cellar's earth walls made it a cool place to store fruit, cheese, milk, and butter.

Rolled hay is lined up beside an old barn. As their riches grew, many Pennsylvanians built barns like this one to support their farming business.

The Pennsylvania farmers built some of the colonies' first big barns to shelter their livestock in winter. The Pennsylvania Germans were especially known for the flowers, birds, and other decorations that they painted on their furniture, barns, and dishes. It may have been one way to make the hard work of farming more beautiful and fun.

Pennsylvania Dutch farmers often painted elaborate designs to decorate their barns.

Another way for farm families to make their lives brighter was to meet with their neighbors often. They gathered for religious services, weddings, and funerals. When land needed clearing, neighbors gathered to cut down trees.

Then they turned the chores of rolling the logs from the clearing and pulling the stumps out of the ground into parties they called frolics. A family that wanted to build a house or barn would invite friends and neighbors for a house or barn raising, also known as a curb-blocking. Working together, the men could put up a building's frame in a single day.

Community Chores

While the men built, the women and children set up a community feast. They would serve soups, sausages, sauerkraut, and potatoes, along with breads, doughnuts, gingerbread, and pies. A family did not need to pay neighbors for their help. The time would certainly come when the helpers would need help in return.

At the yearly butchering time, neighbors would gather at a farm before dawn. The host family would already have huge log fires burning and would have slaughtered their hogs and cattle earlier, scalded the carcasses in boiling water to help remove the hair on the hides, and hung them up. The neighbors then spent the day cutting up the meat. They made sausage and scrapple, which was a mixture of ground meat and cornmeal. They smoked hams and bacon over fires of green hickory chips. Finally, they rendered lard, which meant using a heating process to collect purified animal fat.

The fat would be used later in cooking. After an evening of food and drink, the neighbors went home, carrying with them as much sausage and fresh meat as they needed.

Like children in the city, the farm children were assigned chores, only their chores centered on farm work. The boys learned to plow, plant, and harvest alongside their fathers, while the girls cooked, sewed, gardened, and tended younger children with their mothers. The children all helped in preserving the food grown through the summer for eating through the winter and early spring. Some children learned to read and write in church schools taught by their ministers. In farming season, though, they stopped their schooling and did the work of the farm.

Food of the Pennsylvania Countryside

Americans still enjoy a number of foods that were first introduced in America by Pennsylvania's German settlers.

- coleslaw (*koolslaa*): cold shredded cabbage with a spicy dressing

- sauerkraut: shredded cabbage preserved in brine (strong salty water)

- scrapple: meat left over from butchering cows and pigs that is ground, mixed with cornmeal, then molded, sliced, and fried

- sausage (*wurst*, as in liverwurst or bratwurst): leftover ground meat mixed with spices and salt and stuffed into a skin, or casing

Germans also brought the first waffles to America.

New Business Develops Inland

Although most German settlers were farmers, many of the newcomers had worked in Europe as bakers, carpenters, coopers (barrel makers), tailors, butchers, millers, blacksmiths, and in other trades. From the 1683 founding of Germantown on, skilled German craftsmen set up their shops. The farmers would exchange their livestock and produce for the tradesmen's goods.

As the colony prospered, its citizens no longer had to buy goods from England or the West Indies. Instead, they could buy or barter for most of what they needed from neighbors and local townspeople.

Pennsylvania also had rich natural resources. There was plenty of good land for planting wheat, a crop that needs many acres to grow well. Pennsylvania wheat was an important cash crop (an easily grown and sold crop like cotton or vegetables).

Before farmers could sell the wheat, they needed to grind it into flour or meal, called **grist**. Mills were set up next to streams so the flowing water could power waterwheels. The wheels caused huge stones to turn and grind the wheat. The millers took a fixed amount of each farmer's grist as payment. Much of the wheat produced by Pennsylvania farmers was sold in the form of flour and bread. The region became known as the breadbasket of the American colonies.

Pennsylvania's vast forests provided lumber for building. Like the gristmills, sawmills for speedily cutting logs into boards were built next to fast-moving streams. A sawmill's waterwheel operated the saws, just as the gristmill's wheel turned its grinding stones. Producing lumber became another important business for the colony.

Even more important to Pennsylvania's commerce were its rich deposits of iron **ore.** Local iron was used by black-smiths, coopers, wheelwrights (wheel makers), millers, wagon makers, and farmers. People called iron masters set up "iron plantations" on thousands of wooded acres. Most iron plantations employed a hundred or more people to dig up the ore. The iron was then forged into tools and other useful objects on the plantations.

The Pennsylvania iron business was very successful. As a result, people in England worried that the Pennsylvania iron plantations would take business away from the British iron industry. Therefore, England's body of lawmakers, called Parliament, tried to stop the iron industry in Pennsylvania by making it illegal. The iron masters in Pennsylvania continued to operate anyway.

Blacksmiths were among the most sought-after immigrants.

Safe Haven

One of Pennsylvania's religious groups, known as the Moravians, founded the town of Bethlehem in 1741. The Moravians provided a number of small log houses to help strangers, because they believed that they had a duty to care for the needs of others.

In one log house, the community offered meals. In another, they offered care to sick people. Bethlehem later became known as a place where people could be helped and kept safe during times of war or conflict.

Benefits of Religious Diversity

William Penn's offer of religious freedom for all brought a broad mix of people to Pennsylvania. The Germans, in particular, came from many different religious traditions. Each sect, or group, had its own ideas and its own special talents.

Most of the religious communities arrived and settled as a group. Some of them kept almost completely apart from other groups. However, they still contributed to Pennsylvania's prosperity.

For example, one religious community in the town of Ephrata created a beautiful style of hand-printing and decoration called *fractur*. These people wrote a great deal about their religious ideas. When they decided to publish their writings, they set up a paper mill to make paper and a printing press to print books and pamphlets. Before long, they were supplying most of the paper and some of the best printing in colonial America. They also had the best and largest bookbindery (a place where books were assembled) in the colonies.

The Breadbasket of America

With the help of the most fertile soil in the colonies, the Pennsylvania Germans made central Pennsylvania the breadbasket of America for many years. The Pennsylvania Germans also helped Pennsylvania lead the colonies in education, literature, and the arts. Their influence continues today. After them came another great wave of immigrants. The German settlements would provide a stopping place for these new arrivals on their way to Pennsylvania's western frontier.

CHAPTER FOUR

Rolling Back the Frontier

Merchants, Servants, and Laborers

More and more people arrived in Pennsylvania. Most of them did not share William Penn's religious views. Soon, the Quakers in the colony were greatly outnumbered. When Penn died in 1718, his sons took charge.

Meanwhile, many of Philadelphia's merchants became wealthy. They built large homes and bigger businesses that needed more servants and laborers. Even the Quaker merchants changed some of their ideas about simple living as they became wealthier. They, too, built large country homes and hired servants. Many rich Quakers started dressing in fine clothes that made them look more like members of the British upper class than Quakers.

Immigrants arrived weekly at Philadelphia's busy port.

At the same time, many new settlers pushed west into Pennsylvania's frontier. This angered the Native Americans, whose traditional hunting grounds and villages were being taken. The mutual respect that Penn had established with his fair treatment and careful treaties began to change. Fighting between settlers and Indians would soon become commonplace on the frontier.

The Fastest-Growing City in America

By the early 1700s, Philadelphia was one of the largest, most important cities in the colonies. New, 50-foot-wide (15-meter) roads known as "king's highways" fanned out in every direction from the city. Stagecoach lines that started in Philadelphia carried people, mail, and news all over the colonies. A stagecoach could make it to Lancaster along the new roads in one and a half days. A trip to New York City took two to three days, and a trip to Baltimore, Maryland, took three to four days. Both New York and Baltimore are about 100 miles (161 kilometers) from Philadelphia.

As the city grew, its residents expected more services. For example, they wanted the city to protect them since there were more residents and visitors who might disturb the peace or commit crimes. City leaders appointed watchmen to go out at night "round the town with a small bell…to give notice of the time of the night and the weather." The official description of the watchman's job was recorded in the city archives. It said that the watchmen were responsible "if any disorders or danger happen by fire or otherwise…to acquaint the constables thereof." The constables acted as police officers who could arrest people. The constables and watchmen helped to keep Philadelphia peaceful and safe.

A prison was built, along with a whipping post where people who committed crimes were flogged, or whipped, in public. Across the street stood stocks. People convicted of crimes were locked into these wooden frames by their heads, hands, or feet, in full public view. Both punishments were meant to make the lawbreakers feel ashamed of what they had done.

People who broke the law were put into the stocks.

Fire Departments

In 1736, the Union Fire Company, America's first volunteer fire company, was formed in Philadelphia. Benjamin Franklin, one of colonial Philadelphia's most famous leaders, helped get the company started. Once a month, the firefighters met, according to Franklin, "to spend a social evening together…communicating such ideas as occurred to us upon the subject of fires." Anyone who arrived late or failed to attend had to pay a fine. The fines were used to buy water pumps, ladders, and other fire-fighting equipment.

Fighting fires was a difficult task that required the cooperation of the entire community.

The firefighters took care of their own equipment. The fire buckets were leather. (Leather was used because a wooden bucket could burn more easily, and metal buckets were harder to get.) Each firefighter also had a linen salvage bag, which was used to lower valuables out a window during a fire, and a large basket, in which people or larger items of value could be lowered from burning buildings.

The Fire Mark

The city did not own or run Philadelphia's fire departments, as it does today. Instead, each of the city's insurance companies helped to support one of the fire departments. Each insurance company gave a fire mark—a wooden plaque with a symbol of the company on it—to each family that bought fire insurance. When a fire broke out, the firefighters who arrived on the scene would look for their company's fire mark on the burning building. If the fire mark for their insurance company was not there, they would let the building burn down.

Staying Well

In a city the size of Philadelphia, there were sure to be plenty of people who needed medical care. One of the worst killers of the time was the disease smallpox. Pennsylvanians also caught malaria and yellow fever from mosquitoes that carried these deadly diseases. Rats that had come to America aboard ships spread typhus, which could kill up to 50 percent of those infected with it. A lack of clean water in the city meant outbreaks of typhoid and dysentery, which could both result from drinking dirty water. Many common childhood diseases such as measles, mumps, and the flu spread quickly and could be killers.

Philadelphia's Pennsylvania Hospital, founded in 1751, was the first general hospital in America.

One of Philadelphia's doctors, Thomas Bond, founded America's first hospital for the sick, injured, and insane in the city in 1751. But at that time, there were no vaccinations against deadly diseases, and there was no cure or real treatment, either. Few doctors of the time had medical schooling. No one knew much about diseases or how to treat them. One Quaker doctor humorously described his methods this way:

When patients come to I

I physicks, bleeds and sweats 'em,

Then—if they choose to die,

What's that to I—I lets 'em.

Most people relied on Old World superstitions and traditional family cures to treat illness. Many **almanacs,** which were yearly magazines full of useful information, included remedies that were as likely to harm sick people as to help them.

On Teeth

Colonial Americans were noted for their bad teeth. A visiting Englishman, John Josselyn, wrote that "the women are pitifully tooth-shaken, whether through the coldness of the climate or by sweetmeats [sweets], of which they have a score, I am not able to affirm." His idea of a cure was "brimstone and gunpowder compounded with butter; rub the mandible [jaw] with it, the outside being first warmed." Anyone who had the tools to pull teeth might act as a dentist. A blacksmith, barber, or clockmaker could do the job. Afterward, the "dentist" would craft a false tooth from wood or ivory to replace the one that had been pulled.

Reading in Pennsylvania

Books cost a lot of money in colonial America. Some people, such as Benjamin Franklin, wanted to help people have books to read even if they could not afford to buy them. Franklin had worked as a printer, so he had a special interest in books.

Franklin helped create Philadelphia's first lending library, begun in 1731. A second library was formed in 1746. Unlike the free public libraries that would develop later on, these libraries charged people membership fees, but they still cost less than if people had to buy books.

School Days

At first, the schools run by the Quakers and a few other religious groups were all that were available in Philadelphia. These schools did not have enough room for the city's growing number of young people. Subscription schools, also called "dame schools," made schooling available to more people in towns and cities for about a penny a week from each student. Widows or unmarried women ("dames") taught these schools in their own homes.

Pennsylvania's farm families also wanted their children to be schooled. Often, they invited a teacher to live with one of the families and teach a "neighborhood school" in that farmer's home during the winter. During the growing season, teachers and students alike helped on the farms.

Servants and Slaves

From the time that the colonies were first settled, there had been some Europeans who wanted to come to America but did not have money to pay for the trip. Landowners paid the way for these people. In return, the newcomers became **indentured servants**. This meant that they worked for the landowners until they had paid back what they owed. This usually took five to seven years. During this period, indentured servants worked for their masters seven days a week. They had very few rights and could be punished or imprisoned for not repaying their debts. After their debts were paid, indentured servants were free to work for themselves and own land or businesses. Many masters rewarded their indentured servants with extra clothing, money, or tools to help them start new lives once their debts were paid.

As Philadelphia and other towns grew, many people who had worked as servants went on to other occupations as soon as they had paid off their indentures. They became artisans or bought cheap land for farming. Before long, there was a shortage of servants and laborers in Pennsylvania.

Merchants and traders soon realized they could make money by transporting and selling more indentured servants from Europe or slaves from Africa and the West Indies. By 1750, about half the households in Philadelphia had slaves.

Slaves were treated as though they were animals or possessions, not human beings. Slave traders kidnapped Africans from their tribal homes and brought them to America in slave ships. Once there, the Africans would be sold at slave markets. They became the property of whomever bought them. The buyers, or masters, had complete control over the slaves' lives. The slaves had to do everything they were told to do. They could not possess anything of their own. They could not choose the kind of work they wanted to do, whom they would marry, or where they would live.

A male slave in the city usually worked with his master at the master's trade. The slaves did not have the freedom to leave their masters, but they learned how to do all sorts of jobs. A visitor to the shops in Philadelphia was likely to see a slave working side by side with the master baker, cooper, carpenter, or tailor.

Slaves were often treated badly and given barely enough food and shelter to survive.

Some slaves acted as cabin boys or deckhands for masters on ships. Others worked for manufacturers or cleaned stables and did common labor for tavern keepers. Female slaves worked in people's houses, cooking, cleaning, serving meals, and looking after the children of their masters.

The Life of a Slave

Slavery was especially cruel to families. A child born to slaves automatically became a slave as well. Slaveholders could sell children away from their parents or sell husbands away from their wives. Some slaveholders used harsh treatment and violence against their slaves. Other slaveholders were kinder, yet slaves still tried to run away. No master could be kind enough to make someone want to live in slavery. Some slaves even took their own lives or attacked their masters.

Slaves still had strong family bonds and remembered their African culture. At the slaves' request, Philadelphia's leaders gave them a separate area in the city's Strangers' Burial Ground to bury their dead. This was as close to owning their own land as most of them would come. On Sundays and holidays, they gathered in the cemetery, where they danced their native African dances and sang in their native languages.

Slaves also gathered at the courthouse after work hours to socialize. To do this, they needed passes from their owners. Any slave who was seen away from his or her master without a pass could be jailed and whipped. Quite a few slaves used passes to attend a school for "black scholars" started in the early 1700s.

Life on the Frontier

While Philadelphia was growing and thriving, other settlers tried to make a life for themselves away from the cities. They looked for land of their own out on Pennsylvania's western frontier.

The Scotch-Irish were one such group who spread out across the colony. The Scotch-Irish were people of Scottish descent who had come to America from the northern part of Ireland. Many of them wanted a better life than they had in Ireland. Those who did not have the money for the journey became indentured. Like other groups, the Scotch-Irish brought their religion with them. By 1717, they had established thirteen Presbyterian churches in Philadelphia. Between 1717 and 1776, about 250,000 Scotch-Irish people came to America, and 200,000 of them settled in Pennsylvania.

The Scotch-Irish poured into the Pennsylvania frontier and settled wherever they pleased, whether it was legal or not. They also took land that had never been purchased from the Indians. Unlike William Penn, the Scotch-Irish treated all Native Americans as dangerous enemies. Too often, they chose to kill Indians on sight rather than learn to live peacefully with them. The Iroquois, who lived in that part of the colony, were rightfully angry at such treatment.

Immigrants who settled outside of Pennsylvania's cities often clashed with the Native Americans.

Fear of Indians and close family ties caused the Scotch-Irish to stick closely together. When it came time to build a cabin, neighbors gathered to help. Raising a cabin was a three-day affair. Logs had to be notched, mortar had to be made to hold the logs together, and the chimney needed to be built. The builders would furnish the cabin with built-in beds, a table, stools, and pegs for hanging clothes and other belongings. When the house was built, the proud owner threw a party for everyone who had helped. They often ate, drank, danced, and made music all night long.

The most important crop the settlers planted was corn. They would hand-grind it into meal that could be made into cornbread. The cornmeal might also be boiled with water to make mush that would be served with milk for supper. If the family had no milk, they ate their mush with sweetened water, molasses, or gravy made from fried meat.

Every fall, after the year's harvest, families banded together and traveled to the nearest towns and trading posts. There, they could barter for salt, molasses, sugar, iron, and steel. These were important supplies for the coming year on the frontier.

Tomahawk Rights

For safety, frontier settlers almost always traveled in large groups along the trails the Indians had established long ago. The Native Americans made paths that did not turn to mud in stormy weather. The paths were about 18 inches (45 centimeters) wide, level, and located on high ground.

The trails led the settlers to places on the frontier where they could start their own farms. To claim land, some of the Scotch-Irish exercised "tomahawk rights." A settler would chop down a few trees near a spring and mark the bark of one of the felled trees with his initials. When they saw the marked tree, other settlers would know that this land had already been claimed. Others claimed land by building cabins and raising crops of grain. This was called "taking up." The Pennsylvania government gave a frontier family 400 acres (160 hectares) for taking up.

Homemade on the Frontier

On a frontier farm, the settlers made their own dishes. They carved wood into trenchers (platters), bowls, and noggins (small mugs or cups). Utensils were formed from the gourds or hard-shelled squashes they grew. The settlers also raised flax, a plant with fibers that could be spun into thread. The thread was then woven into homemade cloth, called homespun, from which clothes were made. The settlers traded furs for whatever else they needed. Knives, forks, pots, kettles, plates, salt, and ironware had to be brought out to the frontier by packhorse.

Trouble on the Frontier

Although the Scotch-Irish came from Ireland, they became English colonists when they settled the frontier of Pennsylvania. As they pushed farther and farther west, they stirred up big trouble with Native American tribes by taking the natives' lands. They also moved dangerously close to land claimed by French fur traders along the Ohio River. France was England's enemy. The fight between these two nations to own Pennsylvania's frontier would be the colony's greatest conflict so far.

The Woodland Indians along the Atlantic coast shared a common way of life. They hunted and fished, planted crops, and developed complex traditions and languages. Their close connection to the land is shown though the objects they used every day.

✧ Deer antlers and bones were carved into elaborate combs.

☞ Masks represented spirits and ancestors. They were carved from wood and decorated with human hair, feathers, and bones.

☜ Clothing was made from deerskins. Each tribe had its own unique decorations.

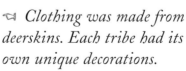

60

Indians

🦆 Reed baskets were woven so tightly that they could hold water.

🕯 The wampum belt, made of tiny shells, was used as money. It was exchanged for goods among Woodland tribes and for furs with European traders.

🕯 Many tasks were done with stone tools. This tomahawk was used in religious ceremonies.
🦆 The arrow heads were for hunting deer and other animals.
🦅 The stone adze was used to hollow out dug out canoes and bowls from wood.

🕯 Many Woodland peoples lived in long-houses. They were made of wood and sod with sloping roofs to shed rain and snow. Entire extended families occupied a single longhouse.

61

CHAPTER FIVE

The French and Indian War

Growing a Colony

Even though the Scotch-Irish frontier settlers created conflict with the Native Americans, most Pennsylvanians remained at peace with the Indians. This was partly because William Penn had always treated the natives with respect. In particular, he had purchased land from them before he sold it to colonists.

Still, the native people and the colonists had different ideas about what it meant to sell land. When the Indians sold land, they thought that they would be sharing it with the colonists. They did not realize they were giving away their rights to the land. The Europeans, on the other hand, believed that buying the land made it their private property.

Native Americans fought alongside the French against the British in the French and Indian War.

The Native Americans began to see that the settlers would take as much land as they could. The Indians also realized they were not going to be allowed to use the land anymore.

In 1737, William Penn's son, Thomas, gave Pennsylvania's leaders a document that he said his father had signed with the Lenni-Lenape in 1686. In this document, the tribe had given a tract of land to the Penns that started at the Delaware River and ran northwest as far as a man could walk in a day and a half. Thomas Penn lied about the document. It was actually an incomplete contract that was never signed by his father or the Lenni-Lenape.

Since no one had actually made the day-and-a-half walk described in the document, the land gift had never been claimed by the Pennsylvania government. Pennsylvania's leaders knew many new people were coming to the colony, and they all wanted land. The leaders decided that the time was right to claim this land, which would later be called the "Walking Purchase."

Thomas Penn decided to cheat the Indians out of as much land as possible. He appointed James Logan, a Pennsylvania official, to see that the exact distance of the Walking Purchase was decided according to the agreement. Logan worked with a native chief to make sure colonists and Indians agreed on the details of the purchase. After that, Logan started playing with the rules of the deal. First, he sent workers to clear the path he wanted to be walked. Then he advertised for the fastest walkers he could find. He promised that whoever could go the farthest in a day and a half would be awarded twenty-five pounds (British currency equal to about $4,000 today) and 50 acres (20 hectares) of land.

Thomas Penn hired men to run instead of walk to cheat the Indians out of their land in the Walking Purchase.

The walkers trained for nine days. When the time came, they took off at a jog. The Indians were furious. As a Lenni-Lenape leader later said, "[The white runners]…should have walked for a few miles and then have sat down and smoked a [peace] pipe, and now and then have shot a squirrel, and not have run, run all day."

Only one of the runners kept going for the full time, covering 64 miles (102 kilometers). This allowed the colony to claim 1,200 square miles (3,120 square kilometers). By measuring the land unfairly, however, the colony's leaders turned the friendly Lenni-Lenape into their future enemies.

Turmoil and Conflict

While the Pennsylvania colonists were busy gobbling up Native American territory, England and France were fighting over land and power in Europe. By the mid-1750s, English and French explorers and settlers had carried their conflict to American soil.

Many Native American tribes were caught in the middle of this fight. They sold land and traded goods with both the English and the French. Now, their traditional homelands were the prize over which the Europeans fought. As the conflict between England and France heated up, the Native Americans began to choose sides. The English were more likely to take Indian land for their settlers, as Pennsylvania had in the Walking Purchase. France was more interested in trade. Therefore, most of the Native Americans sided with France. Since Pennsylvania was an English colony, siding with the French meant siding against Pennsylvania.

Only the Iroquois, who disliked the French, tried not to take sides. They wanted to go on trading with both countries and not fight. This helped the Pennsylvanians, because the Iroquois would have made a powerful enemy. James Logan declared, "If we lose the Iroquois [to the French side], we are gone." Logan knew this was especially true because the Pennsylvania frontier had no defenses. The Pennsylvania government had not approved a **militia**, or local military group, or made any other plans to protect its frontier. For this reason, the colonists hoped that the Iroquois would stay out of the fight.

French Forts

The French depended on waterways that ran through western Pennsylvania to connect their settlements to the north and south. They saw that English settlers in Pennsylvania were quickly moving west, coming too close for France's comfort.

In 1752, the governor of New France (now Canada) sent 2,000 men with tons of supplies to build a string of forts in western Pennsylvania and Virginia. The Iroquois were worried about France's decision to build forts. The natives wanted to be sure that the French would let them continue to have control of these areas. The Iroquois sent a chief known as Half King Tanacharison to speak to the French. He traveled from his home village in New York to the French fort in Presque Isle (near present-day Erie, Pennsylvania).

Tanacharison presented the French officer there with a gift of wampum, a beaded belt, to show goodwill. He requested that both the French and the British leave western Pennsylvania, letting the Iroquois stay and create an area that would separate the European enemies. When the French officer refused, the Indian spoke sternly. "Only send [to the Allegheny region] what we need," he said, "but do not build any forts there.... I shall strike at whoever does not listen to us."

"I am not afraid of flies or mosquitoes," the French commander replied, "for the Indians are such as those....I despise all the stupid things you have said." The French officer then threw the wampum to the floor and kicked it, deeply insulting Tanacharison. From that time on, the Iroquois supported the English.

Protecting the Frontier Families

The frontier people depended on their neighbors in times of danger. They built their cabins as close to each other as they could. Then they erected a stockade, which was a square, cleared piece of ground surrounded by a high fence. It was often located where the boundaries of several farms met.

The stockade walls measured 10 or 12 feet (3 to 3.6 meters) high and were built of upright logs placed one against another. At the corners of a stockade, the settlers built blockhouses from heavy timbers. The blockhouses were special buildings that had no windows at ground level. The second stories had holes that allowed the colonists to shoot their rifles at approaching attackers without putting themselves at risk.

Washington Defends Pennsylvania

By 1753, the Iroquois asked the Pennsylvania government for help against the French. The Pennsylvanians still refused to take action.

In April 1754, Virginia's governor, Robert Dinwiddie, sent a young army lieutenant named George Washington to Pennsylvania with 120 soldiers. Their job was to protect Virginian frontiersmen who were building a fort at present-day Pittsburgh. Before Washington's troops could get there, the French arrived, captured the fort, and claimed it as Fort Duquesne. Washington responded by attacking a small group of French troops. When the French came after him, bringing Native American allies with them, the Americans were forced to retreat. These events started an all-out war.

British Troops Arrive

In 1755, King George II sent Major General Edward Braddock to Pennsylvania with British troops to stop the French from taking over more of the frontier. Braddock knew little about the Pennsylvania wilderness or about the way the French and their Native American allies fought.

Braddock's plan to attack Fort Duquesne turned into a disaster for him and his troops. His wagons got stuck in the mud on the long mountain trails. The French and Native Americans surprised Braddock and his troops as they neared the fort. Braddock and 900 of his 2,500 troops died in the battle. The rest of the troops fled.

Following Braddock's defeat, the British military retreated, leaving western Pennsylvania unprotected once again. Native Americans began to attack settlements along the frontier. They killed some inhabitants, took others captive, destroyed livestock, and burned homes and fields. The settlers fled east, and frontiersmen stormed Philadelphia, demanding protection. At long last, the colony's leaders formed a militia and planned a defense of the frontier. They even offered a reward for Native American scalps.

English Major General Edward Braddock suffered a crushing defeat at Fort Duquesne.

Forced to Action

On April 14, 1756, Pennsylvania declared war on the Native Americans who were attacking the frontier. For the first time, the Quaker colony, which had been so opposed to war, was forced to take action to protect its people. On May 18, England formally declared war on France, and the business of protecting Pennsylvania got serious.

In August 1756, Colonel John Armstrong led a force of 300 Pennsylvania troops in an attack on a major Indian village at Kittanning, on the Allegheny River. Armstrong and his troops rescued eleven American prisoners who had been captured in Indian raids. They also collected at least a dozen Indian scalps. The frontier raids and war parties continued.

Attack and Counterattack

Meanwhile, the war between England and France continued. The English sent Brigadier General John Forbes to Pennsylvania to lead another march against Fort Duquesne. In turn, Forbes asked George Washington's Virginia troops and John Armstrong's Pennsylvania troops to join the British forces.

It was 1758 before Forbes had all his troops and supplies. The troops widened an Indian path so they could travel west. Scouts went ahead to locate the French and destroy any Native American camps. When the scouts were captured, Forbes and the army moved ahead anyway. When they reached Fort Duquesne, they found that the French had burned it to the ground. Then the French had retreated northward toward New France. Forbes took possession of the ruined fort. He called the place Pittsburgh in honor of the British prime minister, William Pitt, and built Fort Pitt there.

Fort Pitt soon became a major center of trade. The trading and troops brought more and more settlers into the region, however, which angered the Native Americans.

Prisoners of the Native Americans

When the Native Americans defeated others in war, they almost always took prisoners. However, carrying sick or wounded prisoners back to their villages made the journey dangerously slow. The Indians would kill such prisoners and scalp them (cut off their scalps). In the Indians' culture, collecting scalps showed their bravery.

If the prisoners, especially women and children, were healthy, the natives often adopted them into their tribe. This was one way of replacing family members who had died in warfare or from disease. There are many stories of prisoners who chose to stay with their Native American "families," even when others came to rescue them later. They had accepted the Indian way of life and did not want to give it up.

The War Moves North

After the French retreated from Fort Duquesne, the war moved north toward New France. In 1758 and 1759, English and American troops won battle after battle. By September 1760, the French had to admit defeat. The French army surrendered to the English commander, Jeffrey Amherst, on September 8.

In late 1758, large numbers of English and American troops began to turn the tide of the war, eventually accepting surrender from the French in 1760.

It took two and half years for the English and French to agree on what would happen to their claims in America. Finally, in 1763, the British and French signed the Treaty of Paris. The treaty officially ended the war between the two countries and declared that France would hand over almost all of the land it controlled in North America to England.

By then, the Native Americans had realized that the British intended to take all Indian lands. That same year, Chief Pontiac of the Ottawa people convinced the western tribes to attack frontier forts in Pennsylvania and Virginia. In the end, however, the fight went on too long for many of Pontiac's followers. They decided to return to their homes and families. Pontiac finally gave up the fight. This opened the way for even more frontier settlement.

CHAPTER SIX

Seeds of Independence

After the War

After the French and Indian War, the people of the frontier no longer trusted their government, because it had done so little to protect them. People's feelings had changed about England, as well. The British commanders in the war had shown little respect for the colonial troops and settlers. This insulted the Pennsylvanians and other Americans and made them dislike the British even more.

Pennsylvania's landscape had also changed because of the war. Military leaders had cleared new roads through the mountain wilderness for their marches to the west. These roads and the roads connecting the Pennsylvania forts made it easier for more settlers to move inland.

The French and Indian War left many colonists wondering why they had fought for the British, who had little respect for their way of life.

As a result of the war, most Native Americans had been pushed farther west. To promote peace with them, the British government promised the Indians that all the territory west of the Appalachian Mountains would be theirs. Parliament told all settlers in this territory that they must give up their claims and move east. However, there were not enough British soldiers to keep the settlers from doing what they wanted. Soon, thousands of new homesteads were set up throughout western Pennsylvania.

The Athens of America

The frontier people of Pennsylvania had suffered horribly through the French and Indian War. The citizens of Philadelphia and the eastern towns, however, were thriving. British soldiers arrived in great numbers. They needed plenty of food, rum, gunpowder, shoes, and warm clothes. Many people in Philadelphia got rich making and selling these items to the soldiers.

Pennsylvania led the colonies in producing wheat, flour, and bread. It was also the top producer of lumber products. Another important product was iron. A visitor to Philadelphia in 1765 wrote, "Everybody in Philadelphia deals more or less in trade." Philadelphia merchants hired ships to transport all these goods to Great Britain, Ireland, the West Indies, and southern Europe. The city's trades depended on seaworthy ships that came and went by way of the Delaware River. In turn, Pennsylvanians bought manufactured goods, mostly from Great Britain. They imported clothing and fabrics, hardware, wire, nails, metal products, books, spices, molasses, coffee, sugar, and salt.

Many people traveled to and from Philadelphia to do business there. To serve these travelers, Pennsylvania had more taverns and inns than any other colony in America. At almost every crossroads, travelers would look for the colorful sign that identified the tavern or inn located there.

Many people in Philadelphia grew wealthy building the establishments that were needed to house and feed the large number of British soldiers that stayed in the colony.

Taverns offered a good night's sleep and refreshment for people and their horses. They also offered entertainment. For example, people could look forward to a game of cards, dice, or backgammon in a tavern. In good weather, there might even be a turkey shoot.

The richer Philadelphia grew, the more like the great cities of Europe it became. Some people started calling it the "Athens of America," comparing it to the famous city of ancient Greece.

New Ideas

In the colonies, peacetime was when people came up with bright ideas for making life easier. In addition to being a leader in the thirteen colonies, Benjamin Franklin became famous as Philadelphia's busiest inventor. He invented

- the lightning rod, which kept buildings from catching fire if lightning struck them

- an odometer, a device that measured how far a mail coach traveled from city to city

- bifocals, a special type of glasses that had split lenses to correct a person's vision for both reading and distance

- an iron stove that heated a house far better than a fireplace

- Franklin's "long arm," a stick with a closable claw on the end that allowed the user to pick up items from the floor without bending over

Some of his inventions are still used today.

Rich and Poor

Philadelphia's wealth was reflected in the clothes its people wore. Farmers and poorer townspeople continued to wear clothing made of wool, leather, linen, and cotton. The wealthy wore taffeta (a fabric that shimmered), silk brocade (a fabric with a fancy woven design), hand-painted Chinese silk, heavy satin, and velvet. Rich people's clothes were decorated with flowered stitching, ruffles, and lace. Instead of a farmer's broad-brimmed summer hat, or a winter hat of fur, fashionable men wore the familiar tricorne (three-cornered) hat.

As people grew richer, they displayed their wealth by wearing fine clothes made of fabric imported from England.

Country women and women who worked as servants wore a white mobcap of gathered cotton. Wealthy women guarded their skin with fancy sunbonnets and long gloves. Children of all classes, once they could walk, were dressed in the fashions of their parents, like small adults.

Pennsylvania's riches provided plenty of goods for the people who lived there. Even poor people and rugged folks of the frontier had much to be thankful for. Trouble was on the horizon, however, as the 1770s approached.

On Wigs

In colonial times, wealthy men, women, and children wore wigs. A wig might be made of human hair, goat or horse hair, hair from calves' or cows' tails, thread, silk, or fine wire. Men wore their wigs over shaved heads. At home, they often replaced their wigs with turbans. (A turban is a piece of fabric wrapped around the head.) Boys wore wigs by the time they turned seven or eight years old.

If a woman chose not to use a wig, she wore her hair in a tall, fancy hairdo. This often meant that she had to sleep with her head on a wooden block so the hairdo would not come undone.

THE JOHN CADWALADER FAMILY, *wearing fancy wigs, was painted by Charles Wilson Peale in 1772.*

The Costs of War

George III became king of England just as the cost of the French and Indian War was added up. King George wanted the American colonists to help pay the cost of the war. After all, the war had been fought to protect them. The best way to collect money from the colonists was to tax them.

In 1765, Parliament passed the Sugar Act. This called for a tax on all sugar, molasses, wine, coffee, and textiles imported into the colonies. Then Parliament passed the Stamp Act, which required the colonists to pay for a special stamp on every type of legal document, as well as on newspapers, almanacs, playing cards, and dice.

The citizens of Pennsylvania were furious about these laws. They felt that these harsh policies took away their rights. Colonial leaders arranged a meeting, the Stamp Act Congress, in New York City. The congress called for colonial merchants to boycott, or refuse to buy, all British goods in order to avoid paying the tax. In Philadelphia, a mob stormed the tax collector's house and demanded that he quit. When the ship carrying the special stamps arrived at Philadelphia's docks, people rioted in the streets. Throughout the colony, people joined the boycott. They gave up the luxuries that were imported from England and lived on what they could produce themselves.

Keeping Warm

Taverns and other public places were rarely heated. To keep warm during Pennsylvania's cold winters, some people carried foot stoves with hot charcoal in them. In the Quaker meetinghouses, pet dogs were allowed to lie at the feet of their masters and mistresses. Large pockets made of wolf fur, into which people could put their feet, might also be attached to the seats. A mother might wrap her baby up mummy-style for warmth.

Homes did not have furnaces. Instead, many rooms of the house had fireplaces for heat. Men, women, and children wore fur-lined boots over heavy, knitted woolen stockings. They put on layers of undergarments made from homespun flannel and outer garments of wool, deerskin, or fur.

The Germans used mattresses stuffed with goose feathers above and below themselves in bed. To stay warm, all the members of a family, and even their visitors,

Teenage boys and girls could share the warmth of the fire, but they had to sit on opposite sides of the room. They could talk privately through a whispering tube.

might sleep in a shared bed placed by the hearth in the kitchen. The bed could be warmed ahead of time with stones or bricks heated in the fire. Sometimes, the colonists used warming pans, which were long-handled, covered containers filled with hot coals. These could be passed beneath the bedcovers to warm the bed. This needed to be done quickly to keep the bed from catching fire.

84

Tempest in a Teapot

Meanwhile, Benjamin Franklin traveled from Philadelphia to London, England, to speak to Parliament. He warned the British government that the colonies would fight for their rights if things did not change. Parliament repealed, or ended, the tax laws in 1766. In turn, the colonists ended the boycott. Then Parliament **adopted** the Townshend Acts the following year. These put new taxes on imported goods, including tea. When the colonies resisted again, Britain repealed all the new taxes except the one on tea.

The Tea Act, passed in May 1773, allowed the East India Company in England to pay no taxes on the tea it sold to the colonies. This meant that it could sell tea more cheaply than the colonists who sold tea in America but had to pay the taxes. Since more people would want to buy the cheaper British tea, the Americans could be put out of business. Once again, the colonists were outraged. In Boston, Massachusetts, in December, a group of men dressed as Native Americans dumped a shipload of East India Company tea into Boston Harbor in protest. This event became known as the Boston Tea Party.

The merchants of Philadelphia decided to refuse the English tea, as well. They demanded that all tea agents, the men who imported English tea, quit doing business.

When the agents refused, crowds of people stormed their homes and forced them to quit. Handbills (small posters) appeared on tavern bulletin boards. The notices threatened the life of any river pilot who brought a tea ship up the Delaware River. When a tea ship docked at the river town of Chester, 10,000 protesters gathered in the yard of the State House, the city building where government leaders met. The people voted to send the ship away, still loaded with tea.

Parliaments' response to the tea-dumping in Boston was harsh. In May 1774, the colonies received the news that the British government would close Boston Harbor on June 1 unless the city paid for the tea that was destroyed. No ships carrying goods, including food, would be allowed into Boston. In addition, Boston merchants would not be able to ship their goods to other colonies or England.

Mail in the Colonies

It was not easy to communicate between one part of the colonies and another. Often, people sent personal letters with friends who were traveling. When Benjamin Franklin was appointed as postmaster general, he worked hard to see that mail traveled as directly and quickly as possible. Letters and newspapers were sent either by stagecoach or by horse riders called post riders. The mail only went out when enough had piled up to make the trip worthwhile. Today, the amount of mail delivered in New York City alone every day equals about the total amount that was delivered in a whole year in the colonies.

In spite of this threat, the Bostonians refused to pay. England also made it legal for British troops to live in people's homes, whether the colonists liked it or not. British commanders could order Boston's citizens to house their troops. Not only did the troops live in the house, the home owner had to feed them at his or her own expense. The colonists called these new laws the "Intolerable Acts."

The Colonies Protest

On May 14, 1774, the people of Boston asked a well-known **Patriot** named Paul Revere to ride his horse from Boston to Philadelphia. He would make a more famous ride a year later to warn colonists that British soldiers had landed in Boston. This time, he carried a letter calling for the Continental Congress, a meeting of delegates from all the colonies, to be held in Philadelphia. At first, Pennsylvania governor John Penn (grandson of William Penn) said no. He did not want to anger Britain by holding this meeting.

Other Philadelphia leaders wrote back, however, to say that they would attend the congress. Thousands of Philadelphia residents turned out to approve the Continental Congress and to appoint six delegates. The First Continental Congress was scheduled to meet in Carpenter's Hall in Philadelphia on September 5, 1774. This meeting would change the course of American history.

CHAPTER SEVEN

The Cradle of the Revolution

To Fight or Not to Fight

The more Americans heard about what King George III and Parliament were doing to Boston, the angrier they became. Some even spoke of going to war against the British.

However, in Pennsylvania, the Quakers did not have much sympathy for Boston, because many Massachusetts leaders had treated Quakers cruelly. Also, the Quakers still did not like war in any form. Furthermore, many Philadelphia merchants worried that they would lose business with England if they went to war against it. The City of Brotherly Love was just not ready for such an extreme, dangerous idea.

◁ *Representatives from the thirteen colonies met in Philadelphia to create and sign the Declaration of Independence.*

The First Continental Congress

On September 5, 1774, fifty-six delegates arrived in Philadelphia for the First Continental Congress. Pennsylvania's delegates expected that the congress would seek a peaceful solution to the problems with England. Others had different ideas.

As members of the First Continental Congress arrived, the people of the busy city of Philadelphia wondered whether a peaceful agreement with England was possible.

The congress asked Philadelphia lawyer John Dickinson to draft a Declaration of Rights and Grievances to be sent to London. In addition, the delegates agreed to another boycott of British goods. They also decided not to sell any of their own goods to England.

Next, every colony agreed to create a system of local committees. The committees would visit merchants to make sure they were obeying the boycott. It was up to the committees to report anyone who ignored the boycott. Such people would have their names listed publicly "to the end, that all such foes to the rights of British America may be publicly known, and universally condemned." The list was meant to shame them for refusing to support the colonies against the British government.

Tar and Feathers

After the First Continental Congress, trouble flared up between people opposed to England (Patriots) and colonists who remained loyal to England (Loyalists or Tories). A form of public shaming called "tarring and feathering" became popular. Patriots would use brushes to dab hot, sticky, black tar all over a Tory's outer clothes. Sometimes the poor fellow was stripped before he was tarred. Then they would stick feathers to the tar and carry the victim around the streets for everyone to see. To avoid being tarred and feathered, many Tories decided it was smarter not to mention which side they were on.

The Second Continental Congress

The colonists had agreed to call another congress if their relationship with England did not improve. By the time the Second Continental Congress met in Philadelphia on May 10, 1775, armed British troops had come to Boston. Battles had been fought, and people on both sides had died. Colonial militia and British troops were now locked in a struggle against each other in Boston. This struggle was the beginning of the Revolutionary War.

The events in Boston convinced the Continental Congress to prepare for war. Each colony started **recruiting** troops to create the Continental army. The congress appointed George Washington as commander of the army and called for six companies of Pennsylvania's expert riflemen to serve under his command. The troops marched to Massachusetts. Meanwhile, Pennsylvanians gathered guns and ammunition to protect Delaware Bay in case of attack.

Declaring Independence

Most of the delegates to the congress did not want the colonies to be independent from England. They thought that Britain's laws were unfair, but they remained loyal to King George.

Crowds gathered outside the site of the Second Continental Congress and argued over what was best for the future of the colonies.

At the Second Continental Congress, John Dickinson wrote to the king, asking him to **repeal** the Intolerable Acts. In reply, the king declared the colonies to be in revolt. Parliament sent 25,000 new troops to America, bringing the total to 40,000. Parliament also outlawed all colonial trade. If colonial ships set sail loaded with goods to sell, the British navy would capture and keep the ships and the goods.

In January 1776, Thomas Paine, a new arrival to Philadelphia from England, wrote a pamphlet called *Common Sense.* In it, he called the king a tyrant and wrote:

"Of more worth is one honest man to society and in the sight of God than all the crowned ruffians [bullies] that ever lived." Throughout the colonies, Paine's *Common Sense* sold 100,000 copies in the first three months after it was published. It convinced many people that independence from England was the only answer.

At first, Philadelphians rejected *Common Sense*. Quite a few Pennsylvania leaders still opposed the independence movement. The Continental Congress, however, voted to declare that the colonies were independent from England.

Thomas Jefferson, a delegate from Virginia, was given the job of writing out a "declaration of independence." In this document, Jefferson wrote "that all men are created equal, that they are endowed by their Creator with certain unalienable [unchangeable] Rights, that among these are Life, Liberty and the pursuit of Happiness." Jefferson went on to list all of the colonists' complaints about the ways the British had mistreated them. Finally, he wrote that the colonies declared themselves free from British rule.

On July 4, 1776, at the Philadelphia State House (the building now known as Independence Hall), the Continental Congress voted to accept the Declaration of Independence. With that act, the colonies officially joined together to form the United States of America.

Fighting on Pennsylvania Soil

Britain was not going to allow the colonies to become their own nation without a fight. The British now planned to capture the colonies' seaboard cities. Philadelphia was high on that list. From Boston, British troops commanded by General William Howe marched swiftly to capture New York City. Washington's Continental army was defeated in two battles on Long Island and in White Plains, New York. Then the British troops marched to Trenton, New Jersey, and finally over the Delaware River into Pennsylvania.

Howe returned to New York for the winter, leaving some troops behind to control Trenton. This put the British very close to Philadelphia. To stay safe, the members of the Continental Congress left Philadelphia and went to Baltimore. Meanwhile, General Washington and a force of only 6,000 men camped just across the Delaware River from the enemy troops in New Jersey. Washington decided it was time to win a battle.

On Christmas night 1776, Washington coordinated a surprise attack at Trenton. His soldiers used small boats to cross the river in a raging storm of snow and ice. The exhausted, freezing troops then marched to Trenton in the early morning hours of December 26 and attacked the British troops there. The attack succeeded, and Washington continued to Princeton, New Jersey, for another victory. The army then settled in for the winter at Morristown, New Jersey, and Washington spent the next several months enlisting new recruits for his army.

The following July, General Howe made his move against Philadelphia. General Washington prepared a defensive line at Brandywine Creek, about 12 miles (19 kilometers) west of Chester. There, on September 11, 1777, the British outmaneuvered Washington's army into a bloody defeat. The wounded soldiers were carried to the **pacifist** towns of Bethlehem and Ephrata, where they received hospital care. The delegates to the Continental Congress, who had since returned to Philadelphia, fled again, first to Lancaster, then to York, Pennsylvania.

Pacifists and War Hospitals

In Pennsylvania, pacifist German-Americans spoke out against the war. Ministers from these groups wrote to Pennsylvania officials, saying that their people would not fight. Instead, they offered to donate money to families who needed help because their men were away fighting.

The Pennsylvania government did not accept the offer. It said the pacifists would have to pay a special war tax or hire substitutes to serve as soldiers for them. Otherwise, they would be charged a fine. The pacifists refused, so the officials took the pacifists' property as payment.

Meanwhile, pacifists helped soldiers who were sick, wounded, or hungry, whether Patriot or Tory. When George Washington took over their community building in Bethlehem as a temporary hospital, the pacifists cared for the sick and wounded.

The Occupation of Philadelphia

Soon, shouts of "The British are coming!" could be heard on every Philadelphia street corner. While some important Patriots fled, most Philadelphians remained. Howe took over Philadelphia on September 26. Under British occupation, the city's Patriot citizens became prisoners. They could not come and go without passes or trade with those who were fighting against the British.

In the meantime, wealthy Tory merchants who depended on the goodwill of England housed Howe and his troops in some of the city's nicest homes. They published Tory newspapers and hosted parties and plays every night. Because Howe had gold with which to pay, many farmers and merchants from outlying areas set aside their Patriot loyalties and sold supplies to the British.

Many colonial troops died during the bitter winter that they were camped at Valley Forge.

While the British were living in luxury in Philadelphia through the winter of 1777–1778, the Continental army was living in crude shelters at Valley Forge, Pennsylvania. It was a freezing winter. The Continental army needed food and clothing, but did not have money to pay for them. Washington lost a large number of his troops to death and disease over the course of that bitter winter. Many others simply ran away, **deserting** the army.

Even so, the awful winter in Valley Forge brought some good news. Spain and the Netherlands, like France, had decided to help the Americans. In addition, some of Pennsylvania's Patriots in the farmland brought clothes and food to the soldiers. New soldiers began to arrive. A German officer named Baron Friedrich Wilhelm von Steuben helped train the new troops and improve their skills as soldiers.

Musical Soldiers

In the days before two-way radios and telephones, the Continental army depended on fife (a small flute) and drum players to be its "tongue and ears." The players were boys, ages twelve to sixteen. Military commanders who needed to send orders to different groups of soldiers over distances used the musicians to "talk" to the soldiers. The beat of the drums told the soldiers how quickly to march. Certain rhythms or tunes might mean "Time to eat," "Turn to the left," or "Stop and rest." In the middle of a battle, the tunes might send the message to attack or retreat.

The British Leave Philadelphia

By winter's end, Sir Henry Clinton had replaced Howe as commander. Then in May 1778, news arrived that France had decided to join the United States in its fight against England. Immediately, Clinton and his troops got ready to leave Philadelphia. They knew the French could sail up the Delaware River and capture the city.

Philadelphia slaves faced a difficult decision. The British treated the slaves poorly but had promised them freedom. However, by this time, Quakers and other Pennsylvanians had begun to speak out against slavery. They said it should be abolished, or ended. The slaves had to decide whether to go with the British or stay in Pennsylvania. Many slaves were willing to take the risk and ran away to join the British. As many as 100,000 slaves throughout the colonies escaped American slavery in this way.

The decision to stay or go was much easier for the Tories of Philadelphia. When the British left the city, about 3,000 Tories went with them. The Tories were afraid of what the Patriots would do to them if they remained.

By the time the British left Philadelphia in May 1778, the Continental Congress was adopting the Articles of Confederation. This document laid out the organization for a new national government.

A Patriot Saves Washington

Lydia Darragh was a homeowner who was forced to let British officers stay in her house. She overheard the officers planning a surprise attack against Washington's troops. By pretending to need flour for baking, Darragh got a pass to travel outside the city. She told what she had heard to an American soldier who promised to pass Darragh's warning along to General Washington. When Howe approached for an attack, Washington and his troops were ready. They ambushed Howe, forcing his army to retreat to Philadelphia.

On the Western Front

In 1778, the British shifted most of their army to the southern colonies. But the fighting was not over in Pennsylvania. The British used their alliance with the Iroquois to fight the Pennsylvanians on the western frontier. In June 1778, settlers had to flee Native American attacks throughout the upper Susquehanna River valley. In July, a violent attack by Indian and British forces in Wyoming, Pennsylvania, led to the Wyoming Massacre. Patriot soldiers were tortured and killed, and settlers were ordered to leave their homes.

For two years, the frontier warfare continued. The winter of 1779–1780, known as "the winter of deep snow," finally put an end to the fighting. As a result of this bitter winter, the Iroquois were too weakened by starvation to ever be a serious threat to the colonists again. The settlers had finally taken the natives' home territory from them.

Women and War

Some women followed their husbands into the army, taking their children along. They worked as army cooks, laundresses, or nurses. Some women followed the men right onto the battle-field. Pennsylvania's Mary Ludwig Hays [McCauley,] nicknamed "Molly Pitcher," was a water carrier. She brought water to the men who operated cannons when they needed to cool their weapons and quench their thirst. When her husband was wounded in the battle at Monmouth, New Jersey, in June 1778, Molly fought in his place until the battle ended. The [McCauleys] both served another seven years in the army.

MARY LUDWIG HAYS [MCCAULEY,] *also known as Molly Pitcher, became a great hero of the Revolutionary War.*

Help From Pennsylvania

Even when the war moved away from Pennsylvania, the colony continued to send troops and assistance to General Washington. Thirteen Pennsylvania regiments and at least as many groups of militiamen served in the Continental army. Pennsylvania had a dozen generals, as well as many other officers, in the army. The iron plantations supplied guns, cannons, and other hardware. Farmers volunteered their wagons and offered their produce. Craftsmen supplied shoes, tools, and other supplies for the soldiers.

When the Patriots won the Revolutionary War in 1783, they owed their success to many colonists, not only those who fought. The Revolution brought the colonial era to an end and marked the beginning of self-government for the United States of America.

CHAPTER EIGHT

A Commonwealth Is Born

When the Bells Rang

John Adams, a Massachusetts delegate to the Second Continental Congress, was in Philadelphia for the reading of the Declaration of Independence in 1776. He described the scene in this way: "The battalions paraded on the Common, and gave us the *feu de joie* [a gun salute in celebration].... The bells rang all day and almost all night."

It was an exciting moment that made people more determined to win the Revolutionary War. The colonists broke away from their mother country and took on the enormous job of creating a new nation. The first step for Pennsylvania, even during the war, was to create a **constitution** that would allow the colony to become a state, or **commonwealth**, and govern itself.

The Liberty Bell became a symbol of American freedom and independence.

105

The Liberty Bell

The Liberty Bell was one of the many bells rung when the Declaration of Independence was read. It had been created in 1751 to celebrate the fiftieth anniversary of William Penn's charter. Its inscription reads, "Proclaim Liberty thro' all the Land to all the Inhabitants thereof." The bell's now-famous crack appeared the first time the bell was rung. The Philadelphians ordered a second bell, but kept the first. During the British occupation of Philadelphia, the townspeople hid both bells so the British could not melt them down to make musket balls. The two bells were rung together for the reading of the Declaration.

A New State Government

In Pennsylvania, people's opinions differed greatly about how the state should be governed. Many people agreed with the views of a group called the Radicals. The Radicals wanted to force anyone who continued to be loyal to England to change or leave. Other people agreed with the Republicans, who wanted citizens to have the freedom to choose their views and their laws. In 1776, the Radicals won the most votes at Pennsylvania's Constitutional Convention and created the commonwealth's first constitution.

Tories and Traitors

Under the Radical government of Pennsylvania, many innocent people were suspected of being Tories. So many people were accused of being traitors that no one knew whom to trust. Mobs attacked anyone they believed had helped the British. People who did not agree with the Radicals' position were fired from their jobs as teachers, merchants, or craftsmen. Some were even forced to pack up their families and leave the commonwealth.

Along with this harshness, however, the Radicals did something that African-Americans had long hoped for. On March 1, 1780, the assembly passed a law that called for gradual emancipation, or freedom, for slaves in Pennsylvania. Although the law did not free Pennsylvania's slaves immediately, it was a beginning. This was the first law of its kind in the United States.

Whether they had been Tories or Patriots, the people of the City of Brotherly Love grew tired of the Radical leaders. In 1782, they elected John Dickinson, who was not a Radical, as president of Pennsylvania. In 1783, the war with England officially ended. Many Pennsylvanians felt that it was a good time for change.

The Stars and Stripes

Legend has it that a Philadelphia seamstress named Betsy Ross sewed the first U.S. flag, the "Stars and Stripes." The Continental Congress, which ordered the flag in 1777, never actually recorded who made up the design. Ross definitely sewed one of the first flags. According to the records kept by Congress, "Mistress Ross" was paid that year for "making ships' colors [flags], etc."

The flag may have been designed by a man named Francis Hopkinson. He had designed the symbol used for the Board of Admiralty. Afterward, he sent a letter to the board demanding credit and "a Quarter Cask of the public Wine" for his work. In his letter, he listed other "Labors of Fancy," which were projects he had decided to do on his own. One of the projects he listed was "The Flag of the United States."

The first United States flag featured thirteen stripes and thirteen stars, representing the colonies that fought for independence.

The board refused to pay, saying that Hopkinson had not submitted a proper bill. Also, Hopkinson "was not the only person consulted on those exhibitions of Fancy, and therefore cannot claim sole merit of them." The flag's design may have come from several people. Maybe Hopkinson just made the board angry by pestering it for payment. Either way, both the flag and the mystery have survived to this day.

New Constitutions

The state government of Pennsylvania grew and changed. The United States adopted the Articles of Confederation in 1781. The articles said that individual states must become part of an American Confederation and "Perpetual Union" and that the rights and privileges of free citizens in one state would apply in all the states. The articles allowed the states to trade with each other. The articles also guaranteed that only the national congress, not the individual states, could declare war or peace.

Members of the Constitutional Convention debated for months and then created the United States Constitution.

However, the articles did not create a strong enough national government for the states. Once again, each state sent delegates to meet in Philadelphia to draft a new document, a constitution. Pennsylvania sent eight delegates. The Constitutional Convention started in May 1787. One of the delegates, Gouverneur Morris, was asked to write the final draft of the document that would become the U.S. Constitution.

All through the summer of 1787, the delegates debated the Constitution. In September, they signed the document and sent it to all of the states for ratification, or approval. Each state then needed to hold a ratification convention. Although Pennsylvanians could not agree on how powerful the new federal government should be, they ratified the Constitution by a two-thirds majority vote in December 1787. Pennsylvania was the second state to do so.

On July 2, 1788, enough states had ratified the U.S. Constitution to make it the new frame of government for the country. New York City became the nation's first capital, where George Washington took his oath of office as the first president of the United States. Afterward, Washington chose an area of land from both Virginia and Maryland to be the nation's permanent capital. While the future U.S. capital was being built, Philadelphia served as the temporary capital. Beginning in December 1790 and for the following ten years, the U.S. government met in Philadelphia.

Philadelphia served as the nation's temporary capital city while the permanent site was being built on land taken from Virginia and Maryland.

In November 1789, Pennsylvania revised its own constitution, basing its new plan on the U.S. Constitution. The new state constitution called for a strong governor, a senate and house of representatives, and a system of judges who kept their jobs for life. All free male citizens who were twenty-one or older and paid taxes could vote. Religious and other freedoms were guaranteed. On September 3, 1790, the new Pennsylvania government assumed its role. Thomas Mifflin was elected as the state's first governor. He had served as president of Pennsylvania during the Revolutionary War and as a general in the Continental army.

For ordinary people in Pennsylvania, many things did not change with independence. They still had to work very hard to survive. However, new inventions soon appeared that would make people's lives easier.

In 1792, the first hard-surfaced road in America was ordered by the Philadelphia Assembly. The road's designer, John McAdam of Scotland, used crushed stone and gravel on ground that had been leveled. This created a surface hard enough that wagon and carriage wheels would not sink into it. The new road allowed a speedy wagon to travel as fast as 7 miles (11 kilometers) per hour on it.

To get water, most people dug wells or built cisterns (large containers for catching rainwater). Then they carried the water indoors, two buckets at a time. Later, some people built systems of hollowed logs to direct water from nearby streams or springs to their homes, farms, and businesses. In 1804, Philadelphia became the first city in America to create a public water system using iron pipes. Even so, it would be many years before plumbing as it is known today became commonplace.

Dirty Business

Without indoor plumbing, flush toilets did not exist. Instead, people used privies, also known as outhouses. A privy was a small, outdoor building that had a bench inside with a hole cut in it. In the city, a man with a horse-drawn cart would come at night to empty the privies. In the country, people often built their privies so that the waste went right into a stream.

People did not want to go outside to the privies at night, so instead, they used ceramic bowls called chamber pots. They stored these under their beds. People at that time did not know much about the importance of cleanliness, so they often emptied their chamber pots right into the street.

New Ideas About Women

Before the Revolutionary War, if girls went to school at all, it was usually to a dame school, which offered basic skills in reading, writing, sewing, patching, and knitting. As U.S. citizens became more concerned about the quality of their future leaders, however, they thought more about the women who might become the mothers of such leaders. Women needed education to raise sons who would be wise enough to be good leaders. At that time, women were not allowed to vote or become political leaders themselves.

People began to realize that it would be good for Pennsylvania if women were educated, too. In 1787, Philadelphia opened the first high school for girls in the United States. At this school, the Young Ladies' Academy of Philadelphia, girls learned reading, writing, math, grammar, geography, music, and catechisms (religious lessons).

Bath Time

During the colonial era and early years of the United States, people did not worry much about being clean. Most people bathed by taking a swim in a river or pond. Otherwise, they simply cleaned parts of themselves with a wet cloth from time to time. One Quaker woman in Philadelphia in 1799 had a shower set up in her backyard. It was probably made from a bucket hung on a rope. She described her first shower this way: "I bore it better than I expected, not having been wet all over at once, for 28 years past."

A New World

Being part of a new nation made Pennsylvanians eager to improve their state and their lives. They began to free their slaves and improve the education of their children. They built better roads and published newspapers and magazines that were carried by the postal system to other states. They made advances in medicine and science. The state continued to serve as America's breadbasket. However, the United States still had much growing up to do. Pennsylvania would remain at the center of growth and progress.

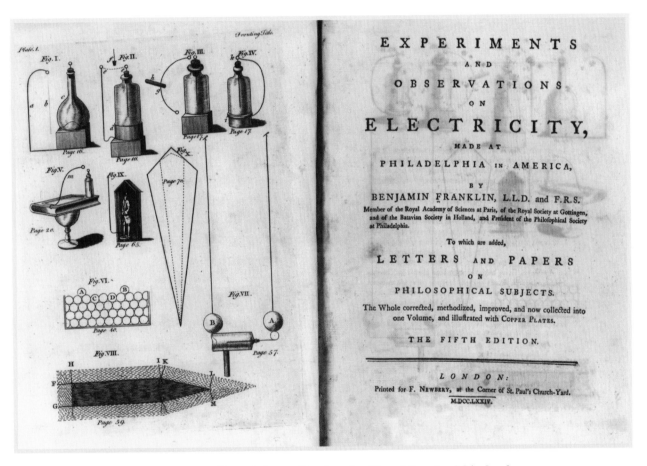

Pennsylvania's leading citizen, Benjamin Franklin, had his book, Experiments and Observations on Electricity, *published throughout the world.*

Recipe
Shoo-Fly Pie

Shoo-fly pie is a traditional Pennsylvania-German treat. The earliest German settlers made this very sweet pie, because the ingredients could survive the long voyage to America. The women often set their baked pies on windowsills to cool. The name is said to come from having to constantly shoo the flies away from the pies as they cooled. This recipe uses a modern oven. In colonial Pennsylvania, the pie would have baked in a wood-burning brick or stone oven.

Modern Version

1 unbaked 9-inch pie crust in a pie pan

CRUMB TOPPING
1 cup flour
1/2 cup brown sugar
1 teaspoon cinnamon
1/2 teaspoon nutmeg
1/3 cup butter

LIQUID FILLING
1/2 cup light molasses
1/2 cup dark corn syrup
1 cup boiling water
1 teaspoon baking soda
1 egg, beaten

- Preheat oven to 325°F.
  Use a hand pastry blender to mix all the topping ingredients until they make fine crumbs. Set the mixture aside.
- Mix the molasses and corn syrup in a bowl. Then stir in the boiling water.
- Add the baking soda and the beaten egg, and mix well. Spoon the liquid mixture into the unbaked pie crust.
- Next, sprinkle the crumb mixture over the liquid in the pie crust.
- Cover a baking sheet with aluminum foil. Place the pie pan, on the baking sheet.
- Put the pie in the preheated oven. Bake it for about forty minutes or until the pie is set (solid) and dark brown.

Shoo-fly pie tastes great warm or cool and topped with fresh whipped cream. Setting it on a windowsill is optional.

This activity should be done with adult supervision.

Activity
Fraktur

The Colonial American Fraktur is a form of folk art. *Fraktur,* means "fractured writing" in German. Colonists recorded birth certificates, songbooks, and other documents as Frakturs. The writing was fancy and elaborate. Colorful flowers, deer, unicorns, fish, and snakes were all popular symbols found on Frakturs. This artwork added color to the home while recording key family events.

Directions

White paper (8 1/2 inches x 11 inches)
Tracing paper (4 3/4 inches x 6 1/2 inches)
Tea bags • Water • Rectangular pan
Calligraphy pen
Colored pencils, crayons, paints, or pens

- Soak the tea bags in water in a rectangular pan until the water turns brownish or "tea colored."
- Soak a sheet of white paper in the liquid until it is dyed a tea color. Remove the paper and let it dry overnight. (The longer you leave the paper in the tea mixture, the darker it will become.)
- Draw a border on the tea-dyed paper about an inch from each side. Decorate the border by drawing geometric shapes or figures within it and coloring them.
- Use a ruler or compass and a pencil to lightly draw an oval, rectangle, or circle on the tracing paper. Cut out the shape, and trace around it in the center of the tea-dyed paper.
- Draw animals, flowers, birds, or other designs around your traced shape. Color the designs.
- Practice writing the content for your special event on scrap paper. Use fancy writing or elaborate letters.
- Use the calligraphy pen to write the final copy inside the shape. Erase pencil marks.
- Add further decoration, if you like.

This activity should be done with adult supervision.

PENNSYLVANIA
Time Line

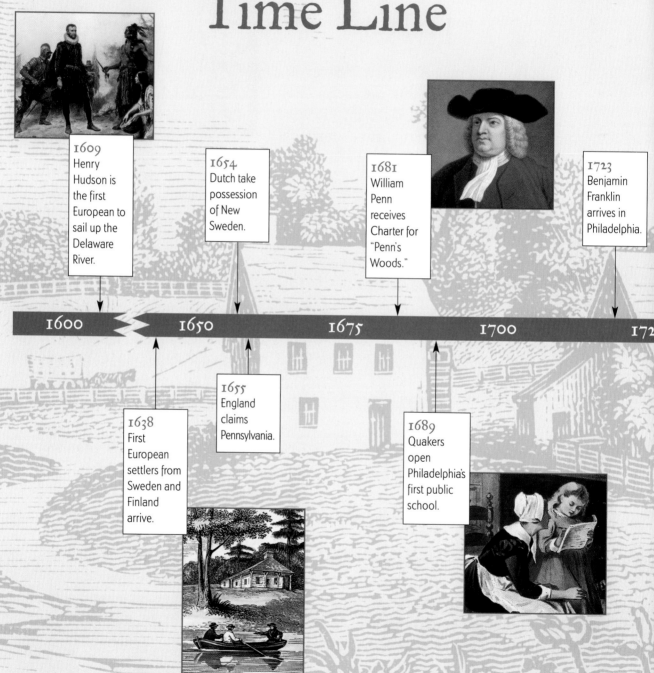

1609
Henry Hudson is the first European to sail up the Delaware River.

1654
Dutch take possession of New Sweden.

1681
William Penn receives Charter for "Penn's Woods."

1723
Benjamin Franklin arrives in Philadelphia.

1600   1650   1675   1700   172

1638
First European settlers from Sweden and Finland arrive.

1655
England claims Pennsylvania.

1689
Quakers open Philadelphia's first public school.

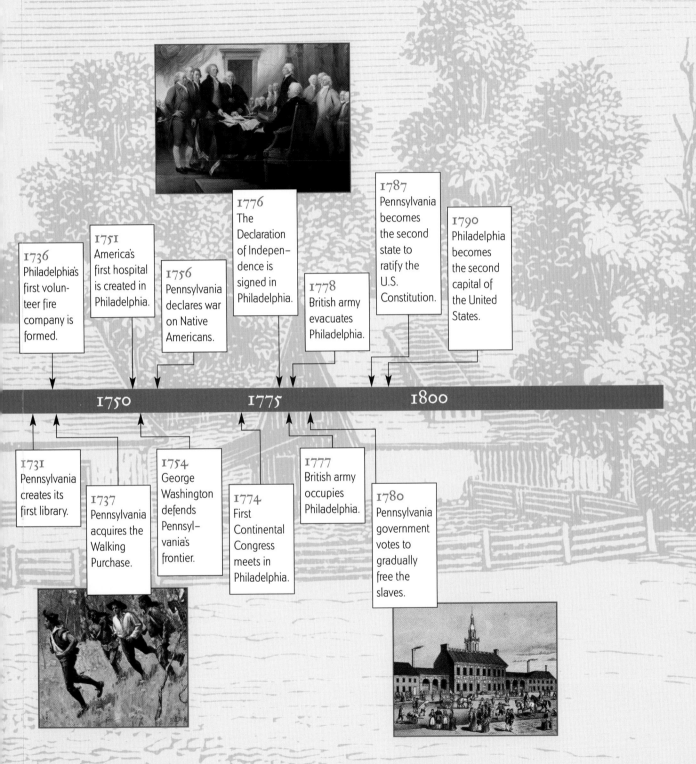

1736 Philadelphia's first volunteer fire company is formed.

1751 America's first hospital is created in Philadelphia.

1756 Pennsylvania declares war on Native Americans.

1776 The Declaration of Independence is signed in Philadelphia.

1778 British army evacuates Philadelphia.

1787 Pennsylvania becomes the second state to ratify the U.S. Constitution.

1790 Philadelphia becomes the second capital of the United States.

1750

1775

1800

1731 Pennsylvania creates its first library.

1737 Pennsylvania acquires the Walking Purchase.

1754 George Washington defends Pennsylvania's frontier.

1774 First Continental Congress meets in Philadelphia.

1777 British army occupies Philadelphia.

1780 Pennsylvania government votes to gradually free the slaves.

119

Further Reading

De Angeli, Marguerite. *Skippack School: Being the Story of Eli Shrawder and of One Christoper Dock, Schoolmaster About the Year 1750.* Scotsdale, PA: Herald Press, 1999.

DeFord, Deborah, and Harry Stout. *An Enemy Among Them.* Boston, MA: Houghton Mifflin, 1987.

Knight, James E. *Seventh and Walnut.* Mahwah, NJ: Troll, 1999.

Knight, James E., and Karen Milone. *The Farm.* Mahwah, NJ: Troll, 1998.

Lutz, Norma Jean, and Arthur M. Schlesinger, Jr. *William Penn: Founder of Democracy.* Langhorne, PA: Chelsea House, 2000.

Richter, Conrad. *The Light in the Forest.* New York, NY: Fawcett Books, 1991.

Glossary

adopt to accept and carry out the terms of a law or an act

almanac a booklet published once a year that contained predictions about the weather and the next year's crops

apprentice someone who works for another person for a specific amount of time in return for instruction in a trade, an art, or a business

barter to trade by exchanging one thing for another instead of using money

charter an official, written document from a king or government that guarantees certain rights

commonwealth a political unit such as a state or nation

constitution a set of laws that are used as the legal standard for a state or country

desert to abandon or walk out on military service without permission

feud an ongoing clash between family members or people on opposite sides of an issue

grist a batch of grain for grinding, or the flour or meal that it becomes after grinding

import to bring into a place or country from elsewhere

indentured servant a person who agrees to work for another person in exchange for having travel expenses paid and basic needs supplied

militia man army made up of ordinary citizens instead of professional soldiers

ore a mineral that contains a valuable metal, such as iron

pacifist a person who does not believe in violence or war as a way to settle conflict

Patriot in the American Revolution, someone who sided with the colonists fighting the British

potash a white salt found in wood ashes that was used to make lye soap

recruit to enlist new members to join a cause

repeal to revoke or take back

troops a group of soldiers

Index